Your Video Playbook

How To
Demonstrate Your Value
Through Video

Pat Ferdinandi

Paraphrased from *Hamlet* by William Shakespeare:

To video, or not to video: that is the question:
Whether 'tis nobler in the mind to miss
The opportunities of outrageous fortune,
Or to take arms against the tides of change,
And by opposing end them? To allow my business to die or
sleep
No more; and by a sleep to say my business ends.

To Be Or Not To Be Video

Your Video Playbook: How to demonstrate your value through video.

(link address provided in Hyperlink Table at the end of the book)

Pat Ferdinandi's Your Video Playbook

The author may be contacted at the following address:
Viditude
PO Box 638 Montclair, NJ 07042 USA
Phone: 973-509-9427
Email: TalkToUs@Viditude.com
Website: Viditude.com

ISBN-13: 978-1463517205

First Printing, June 2011

Library of Congress Cataloging-in-Publication

Data available upon request.

making sure your videos are creating a lot of talk.

this book is dedicated to

growing your business

through video

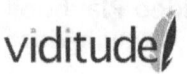

Acknowledgements

No book is developed without the assistance of so many others. A good book is a based upon those who help or have educated me with their own writings. It takes a group of special people to inspire, critique, and suggest things that bring the entire project together. This project is no exception. Allow me this page to personally thank people who have supported me while writing this book:

- ▶ My wonderful husband, Giuseppe, who is Scarlet's favorite caretaker.

- ▶ My sister, Karen Smith, who corrects my bad grammar on so many of my word-works *(don't blame her for what I forgot to correct).* And when she gets stuck...off to my mother, Louise Smith, who (@ 93) proves every day that age has nothing to do with what your mind can conceive.

- ▶ Colleagues that are also GREAT storytellers with great insight: Tom Cagley, Mark Cohen, Caryl Felicetta, Tommy Hilcken, Tracy Glock, Tom Graves, Donna Hook, Chris Kieff, Peter Lipa, Ed McLaughlin, Joe Micara, Jacob Peck, Igor Perchuk, Sue Pirog, Robert Thames, and Kevin Thompson.

- ▶ Fellow TriIibers *(Seth Godin's private social network)* for tweaking the tweets in this book & helping to make this squawkable.

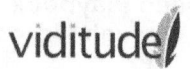
- My Heroes & Mentors: <u>Patricia Fripp</u>, <u>Steve Garfield</u>, <u>Jeffrey Gitomer</u>, <u>Seth Godin</u>, <u>Kevin Naltz</u>, <u>Gideon Shalwick</u> & <u>Alan Weiss</u>.

- *And to all readers, listeners, and viewers...may each idea help you demonstrate your value through video!*

Act 1: What Will Video Do for You

Creating videos has never been easier. Social media has reached a level of sophistication to enable you to reach existing and potential customers with ease.

So, it's easy? Is video right for you or your business?

The Power of Video Today

Let me introduce you to Snowball...a sulfur-crested cockatoo.

Image from BirdLoversOnly

(link address provided in Hyperlink Table at the end of the book)

His caretaker could no longer meet his demands. The caretaker found a local <u>parrot shelter</u>. As the caretaker was leaving, he gave Irena Schulz a CD, "If Snowball acts up, play this song...sit back...and watch. He calms down after dancing."

Not long afterwards, Snowball started screeching for attention. Irena put on the CD of the <u>Back Street Boys</u>™ and could not believe what she saw. She was so amazed, she took her <u>Flip video recorder</u>[1] and recorded Snowball's dancing ability. She placed the <u>video</u> on YouTube **for free**. She emailed the link to the video to all her parrot-loving friends...who passed the link to other friends...who passed the link to other friends...the passing continued. In three years, Snowball's video had over 4 million views on YouTube!

Heck, if a <u>sulfur-crested cockatoo</u> can dance his way to over 4 million views in just 3 years, why can't a 3-5 minute video work for you? Because of <u>Snowball's video</u>, this beautiful sulfur-crested cockatoo parrot has been on <u>several TV shows</u>, part of 3 <u>scientific papers</u> on how the brain works, <u>a Taco Bell Commercial</u>, has related <u>t-shirts</u>, mugs, and other products that have been increasing in sales for the <u>BirdLoversOnly</u> charity since the video of him dancing to the Back Street Boys aired 3 years ago. Donations to the <u>BirdLoversOnly</u> 501c, in Irena's own words, "started coming in *like water*".

---

[1] Cisco announced the discontinued Flip line in April, 2011. To give credit, the Flip camera initiated the DIY Video market. The combination of YouTube and the Flip revolutionized your business opportunity. In less than four years, the Flip was replaced by smart phones and other mini-video recorders.

Are You Part of the Community

Every year, more people are shopping online and more people do research via the internet. The word of mouth advertising is now all about online conversations through Facebook, Twitter, Squidoo, LinkedIn, FourSquare, SlideShare, Flickr, and YouTube and millions of other sites. Communities are built around discussions about products, services and people. Wish list ideas are discussed between your customers and potential customers. What are they saying about **you**? Are **you** part of the community? Are **you** listening?

Every year, job applicants are being found through online searches. A prospective employee's LinkedIn profile and Facebook pages are reviewed. Employers and colleges are using video for student selection. It's about content. It's about who knows you. It's about the conversation you lead around your specialty. Are you participating in the discussion? Are you providing ideas others appreciate and talk about with others? Are you initiating collaboration and leading the discussion towards solving key problems?

Are you part of the **social media** community?

Today it's not who you know ... it's about who knows you and how they **feel** about you as expressed online. People want to see you in action. People want to feel an emotional connection. People want to see the type of emotional connections others have and share with and

about you. Today...it's about adding video to help spread the word about you!

Your Opportunity

The world has changed. No longer are people willing to just hear you say you are the best. People want to see proof. People want YOU to earn their trust by providing what they consider valuable (**perceived** value). The more you are trusted, the better your chance will be to earn the right to build a relationship with individuals and build your continual sales funnel.

Videos are a great way to display value and initiate a relationship with multiple followers. Videos can illustrate what you do with a series of "how to" videos or a video that contains testimonials from your customers, or interviews with experts and colleagues in your field. It's an ideal way to build a community around you and your brand. And did I mention...FOR FREE!

Today, more people watch a video than read. In fact, one-minute of video is worth about 1.8 million words. How's that for a comparison!? So, your how-to instruction booklet will ONLY be read after they trust you...after they see you in video. Videos are believed more because they provide the information with an emotional connection. You can't display your smile, your bright eyes; your enthusiasm on paper as well as you can in video.

Need more statistics?

- According to a 2009 research paper by Nate Elliott, Forrester Research, <u>videos are 53 times</u> more likely to be on the 1st page of Google results!
- Videos <u>raise the click-through rate</u> in emails.
- As early as 2008, YouTube became the <u>2nd largest search engine</u> in English speaking environments!
- <u>A study from May 2010</u> by Daniel Ruby of <u>Chitika</u>, an online advertising network of 100,000 sites, found that, on average, 34 percent of Google's traffic went to the No. 1 result, about twice the percentage that went to No. 2.
- YouTube, <u>at Social Media Week 2011</u>, said YouTube was averaging 2 BILLION views per day!
- <u>MeFeedia</u> reports in March of 2011 that traffic from mobile devices to view video is now 5 percent (up from 1 percent last years). This figure is based upon MeFeedia indexed about 30 million videos from more than 33,000 video web sites.

What You Need To Do Now

Let's face it; none of us has time to waste. Keeping up with our reading, writing, watching, or videoing gets more and more difficult...and for those we want to reach. Trying to keep up with blogs, online magazines, websites, Facebook, LinkedIn, Twitter, FourSquare, Slideshare and YouTube is becoming overwhelming. It is just too much to consume...for you and your audience.

<u>Viditude</u> developed this simple <u>7 P's methodology</u> to help you get the most out of your time, effort, and reach from your videos. The key is to focus on your customer and

client audience so they get enthusiastic about spreading the word about you because you have **"perceived"** value (value *they* want...not what *you* think is of value).

Everyone has the same 24 hours. My goal is to make yours the most productive by providing tips I've learned through my own trial-and-errors AND through leaders in sales, marketing, videoing, and social media. I'm not bashful. I'll be sharing some of my not-so-good videos to talk about lessons learned. You will be able to learn from my mistakes and take a big leap ahead of your competition.

What you need to do now is keep an open mind...read through this book...watch related videos...act on them...and be ready for your increased opportunities!

Eliminating Your Fears

I hear these excuses ALL THE TIME! You may have used them yourself. Well...let's get them out on the table so you can be successful by leaving them behind.

> ***I don't use social media.*** Why not? It's not going away. In fact, more people are using the Internet to find out about anything today than yesterday. Social Media is now taking over search engines for word of mouth (now called *"word of mouse"*) advertising, promotion, and recommendations. The current order of social media presence is: Facebook, YouTube, Twitter, LinkedIn (linked with SlideShare), Blog (as the landing page) and the secret weapon Squidoo. I'll

show you how to make your video available on each website and how to best initiate the **word of mouse** about you!

I'm afraid of being on camera. Public speaking is among the top ten fears of all time. Let's get that thought out of your head now. You are NOT giving a speech. You are having a conversation with people you are passionate about helping. It's just through the lens of a video recorder. Viewers are NOT watching your video to be entertained by a six-figured keynote speaker. Your audience is watching your video to *learn* something. If you have passion for what you do and you know your topic, you will come across natural on camera. If you keep in mind it is about sharing what others want to know (*their* "perceived" value), you are doing your customers a disservice by not providing it via video.

I don't know what to say. Yes you do! You are just allowing yourself to get overwhelmed by all the different topics you can talk about. Make a list of potential topics. I provide questions in a later section in this book to help guide you. As a brief introduction, make each question specific. For example: how to pick the right apples or how to pick the right workout gear for sub-freezing temperatures. Each topic can be a video. Prioritize your list by what you feel most comfortable talking about for one to three minutes. That's it, one minute. Now, record your video. It will get easier as you go. This book will help you step by step. The important point is to get started.

I'm boring. No you aren't! Everyone has charisma. It does vary in degrees. Your goal is to recognize you have it and use what you've got. A very serious person talking about a very serious topic can provide a charismatic video. It's about finding and sharing your passion. Providing valuable insights on your passion comes across as authentic. People connect with authentic individuals. The right level of charisma will come through. I'll provide some speaking tips later to improve the display of your charisma on video.

I don't have time to create a video. Time isn't the issue. Everyone has the same amount of time as everyone else. You just haven't placed video high enough on your priority list. That may be from fear, not knowing how to get started, or not knowing what to do. This book will help you get it done. However, you do need to make a commitment to yourself to spend *just 15 minutes daily* thinking about how to demonstrate your value through video. Begin by reading this book for at least 15 minutes a day. The same approach to writing a book, applies to creating videos to increase your following. YouTube has over 2 billion views a day. This book will help **your** video be one of them.

I'll look like an idiot! No, you won't. You just need to learn a few speaker tips and focus on providing value. You already have the skills. You just need to be reminded on how to record a few takes, and raise your confidence. Video is here and YOU can use it to

add perceived value to your audience—which can lead up to 30% increased sales.

What if people criticize me on the public Internet? It is impossible to please everyone. Amazon knows every book will have at least one five-star and one one-star rating. What drives people to buy is the pattern. If you have more four-star reviews, people will believe the reviews (Likes (👍)

versus Dislikes (👎) in YouTube and Facebook). You may find some nasty people out there who will be negative. That's life. The good news is the people who will support you. If someone attacks you, your EARNED loyal following will come to your rescue. Some of your videos will be a hit; some will flop with no comments. It's the overall pattern of providing value that builds relationships, loyalty, trust, a following, and sales.

I'm technically challenged! Creating video has become so easy with new cameras and sites like YouTube. It's as easy as point-shoot-edit-upload (with edit being optional). The world of video doesn't require expensive equipment, software, stages, actors, professional scriptwriters, videographers, or producers. You may wish to grow to that level *(or hire someone for part of the effort)*. It's just so easy to begin with a DIY: Do It Yourself approach. After all, no one knows your message, story or have the level of passion as you do. This book will cover the basics

to get you started. After you try it yourself, you can bring in others to help you take it to the next level.

My business is doing well without video! Congratulations! Our next question is, how much **more** could you be making or how many more loyal customers could you get and retain by adding video to your brand? I've seen sales increase 30% in some cases by adding video. I've seen customer attrition drop by 20% because video built a stronger loyalty bond. Are you averse to making more profit? If you don't know what to do with the extra business, I'm sure your kids or your favorite charity (some are listed at the end of this book) would appreciate the extra donation. Just try using video for 6 months, see if you notice an uptick. Then send me an <u>email</u> with your results. I'd love to hear about it.

I already use video and it has had minimal impact given the time and money I've invested. It's time to take a close look at what videos you created. It's time to ask your customers or clients what information they would find valuable (*customer* perceived value) and create a video sharing that information. It's time to look at your presentation style, your stage, and how you are promoting yourself. That is what makes this book different from others. This 7 P's methodology playbook will take you through the thinking and executing steps to demonstrate your value through video! It combines three key elements of success: Social Media, Presentation Message, and Video tips. It's the

combination that may tweak your approach and make the difference to your success.

It's time to stop the excuses and start demonstrating your value through video. As a speaker specializing in social media storytelling, I know you will grow in sales, community, knowledge and confidence. You can do it. Just take one step at a time. Read and act out each scene and be prepared for the opportunities. Nike™ was right..."Just Do It!"

Act 2: The Viditude 7 P's Playbook

You already know what you need to do now...you need to start planning your video strategy for yourself, product, or company. NOW!

What you are looking for now is how to go about doing it!

Ah, that's the purpose of this small book (yes, in text form) with video. It's for the DIY's (Do it Yourself-ers) who want to bring attention to their message, product or service. I am going to hold your hand to help you get the most out of your videos. I will discuss the 7-step process used by Viditude to get you going. It has worked for me personally over and over again.

1. *Plan:*   Know your story, strategy, objectives, and goals.
2. *Prepare:* Know what you want to say.
3. *Practice:* Tweak your speech or requests for testimonials.
4. *Present:* Check your environment, stage, and appearance.
5. *Produce:* Edit to a concise nub. Add helpful features to enhance the experience of your viewers.
6. *Post:*   What to include when you post your video to increase "findability".
7. *Promote:* Start the ball rolling by feeding the "mouse" to spread the good word about you.

Scene 1: Plan

I've been involved in multiple careers, industries and focus-areas. I've learned about strategic planning, business architecture, business models and taught others to do the same (and I am still called in to help). I can tell you that things work better when you think it through first!

This doesn't mean you need to stick to the plan 100%. You will learn as you go and make adjustments. It does mean that the steps I am going to discuss in this section will help you develop the roadmap to success. In terms of *you*, planning will clarify who you are, what you want to achieve, and how to achieve it:

a. *Your Purpose:*   Who will your audience see?
b. *Your Story:*   What will your audience connect with?
c. *Your Objective:*   What will be you're desired outcome (business and video)?
d. *Your Goals:*   What milestones are you going to set for yourself to keep you going?
e. *Your Strategy:*   How are you going to demonstrate your value through video?
f. *Your Plan:*   What action steps are you going to take to get your videos out and noticed?
g. *Your Success:*   How will you measure your impact?

Your Purpose: Why Do You Do What You Do?

It's time to take a close look at yourself. Your video is about YOU. The question is... who are you?

I'm sure you can tell me what you do. You can probably describe, in excruciating detail, how to do it. Let me ask you a simple question. **Why** do you do what you do?

Sorry, just making money isn't enough. Money is a result, and many times a meaningless metric. It is a temporary manipulative tactic to get sales. I've seen companies lower and lower prices to make sales with the result of no profit. There is no customer loyalty when the relationship is based on price. It is hard to break loyalty when a customer believes in what you believe. They connect **emotionally** to your passion.

Image from Simon Sinek Website
(link address provided in Hyperlink Table at the end of the book)

There is no emotion in money. Yes, not having money is a de-motivator...but working for money is never enough to sustain the motivation to make a difference. Motivation is sustained through inspiration. Inspiration is based upon belief in yourself and a cause. A belief is emotional—a connectable and spreadable emotion!

Here is a video by Simon Sinek for his *Start With Why*

book. Watch his video to understand the purpose of starting with Why. His video will help you to think about your core and create a video based upon what is emotionally important to you.

People connect emotionally before they do analytically. In fact, people will first connect emotionally and use their analytics to find a reason (convince themselves) to buy you, your product/service or company. It requires being clear and concise about why you do what you do for others to connect. Mixed messages never connect.

There may be hundreds or even thousands of businesses that do what you do. How are you the same? What makes you different? Again, being the cheapest will not get you a following. Are you passionate about that difference? That difference needs to be something audiences want to squawk (aka shout) about to others. It is that difference which begins to build the individual relationship with your audience and soon a community who will spread what you say (remember Snowball and the parrot community's involvement). It is that difference, rooted in your passion, which must come across in your videos.

For those of you who saw the movie <u>City Slickers</u> ... you will remember this dialog. Curly Washburn *(played by Jack Palance)* told Mitch Robbins *(played by Billy Crystal)*:

Curly: "Do you know what the secret of life is?"

[holds up one finger]

Curly: "This..."

Mitch: "Your finger?"

Curly: "One thing. Just one thing. You stick to that and the rest don't mean shit."

Mitch: "But, what is the **one** thing?"

Curly: [smiles] "That's what **you** have to find out."

What is that ONE thing you can call your own? The "one thing" that explains you? What is that one thing you are passionate about? What is that one thing that makes you remarkable...that will connect emotionally with your audience? Is it:

▶ customer service?

▶ listening to your customers?

▶ helping customers solve a problem?

▶ helping them look their best?

▶ your product or service?

▶ your love of what you do?

▶ the success of your customers!

Write your "one thing" down on a post-it™ note. Post it on your bathroom mirror, your desk phone, and your computer. Post it so you keep your "one thing" in front of mind.

Your Core Message: What Story Will Stick

All your stories need to convey that one passionate element which connects with your audience. It will be the theme from the first video through the entire set you will produce. Let's use my management consulting work as an example:

> Years of profitable consulting was based on Pat's strong belief. All ideas are achievable when the ideas are clarified *(her one passion)*. Her one *(remarkable)* gift is her ability to translate thoughts and ideas into something actionable *(perceived value).* She has been able to build her *(emotional)* connections through her contagious enthusiasm which inspires *(action)* motivation in everyone with her easy to follow, step-by-step explanations.
>
> This comes through in every video where Pat appears, and in all the videos she coaches others to create. Because she believes in the project, she will translate or script the story for the audience to connect and talk about.

You can build the basis of your repeatable story (a story spread by your following over and over again) by identifying:

- ▶ What is your passion?
- ▶ What remarkable gift do you have which is different from your competition?

► What does your audience value that you can provide them?

► What will be the action you want your audience to take after watching your video?

Marketing studies show it usually takes at least six repetitions of a message for it to register with prospective customers. Video allows you to continually convey your message 24/7.

Your Story Characters: Who Are the Main and Secondary Characters

Every story has multiple characters. The main character(s) is someone others can relate to on an emotional basis; someone who inspires or motivates action. This character is YOUR customer or audience demographic. It is a sampling or composite of your existing customers and why they work with or buy from you. These individuals or companies must be the star of every video. Each customer wants to watch your video as if he or she is looking in the mirror. He or she wants to see something of him or herself in the main character and the situation *(aka story).* Your main character is someone who:

1. wants to learn in a fun, entertaining way
2. has a situation requiring resolution
3. loves the topic you are talking about
4. wants to determine if you are someone he or she wants to do business with you

Think about your demographic. Describe in detail who is your typical customer. Here are some of the many descriptors you can use to define your customer and main character.

► Age range (20-30s, Gen-Xers, AARP members)
► Sex (more females drop off the laundry for themselves than men)
► Household Income Range ($50k to $75k)
► Living Arrangement (single, couple, group, house, apartment, rent, own)
► Location (radius, towns, national, international, internet)
► Situation (stop by before food shopping, pre-theater snack, doctor insists he or she lose weight)
► Interests (hobbies, sports teams, career, faith)

Now that you have a good visual picture of your main character, let's look at which style would fit your demographic. There are five styles of videos *(for which you will create multiples of each)*:

► *Testimonials:* A customer or colleague saying WHY they do business with you. They are describing their **perceived** value and eliminate potential client objections. Every testimonial is provided by a person who fits the demographic of your typical customer. Think about the fringe as well as right in the middle. I'll discuss later strategic questions you can ask yourself to increase your customer focus.

▶ *How-To/Demonstration:* You are teaching a customer or colleague how to do something related to your knowledge. Begin with a situation the viewers can relate to in their own lives on an emotional level. These can be instructional (how to make a cake) or demonstrations (how to use the cake mixer). Demonstrations means explaining what you do or your product in terms of how your product or service will be of value to your customer relative to what your customer perceives is valuable. You will be covering any potential objections the audience may have in doing business with you. You are reducing the risk of doing business with you. This type of video is used to demonstrate your knowledge and skill (and willingness to be helpful) to your demographic ...thus leading to credibility, trust, and loyalty. Think of your character's demographic for situations to demonstrate knowledge and spark ideas.

▶ *Informational:* These are providing information...not selling. Informational does just that. It provides information about a favorite topic (historical facts or reviews) or seeks information about a topic from your customers. Informational type of videos is used to demonstrate your knowledge...thus leading to credibility, trust, and loyalty. What is changing in your industry your customers may be curious about or need to know to stay fresh? What trends impact your industry and eventually your customers (technical, lifestyle, regulatory) or

prospective employers? Think of your character's demographic for interests or would they may want to know for ideas. For example, a real estate broker may provide a video on *how to de-clutter your home for sale*.

▶ *Interviews:* You lead the discussion by interviewing a colleague, customer, or expert in your area. It's easier than you think. You just need to be prepared with questions. Your value is your ability to reach people your customers can not. Think about your character's demographic for interests and their specific situation for ideas. If you can get a big player to interview, the interview can be a form of endorsement. This endorsement will help build your audiences trust in you.

▶ *Promotional* is the advertisement. You can be announcing a new product or service. You may be announcing a contest. You may be announcing a special event. The difference between the previous how-to and a promotion video is one of *helping* versus *alerting* your followers. Followers are prospects and people who you've already converted to a customer. These customers may want to be an "<u>early adopter</u>" of what you have to offer. This demographic usually wants to be first in line to purchase the latest thing (picture the customers waiting in line the night before the latest Apple product is released). Incorporate the use of words commonly used by your characters in their demographic. Keep in mind the compelling

EMOTIONAL reason for a customer to continue to use your product/service, that is NOT available by your competitors. If seasonal, create the video using the right stage. Create a seasonal environment and music, if appropriate. For all promotional videos, ensure you have a "squeeze page" or landing page for your customer to BUY what you are selling.

The promotional advertisements which work best are those who provide information as well. Consider the video more of education + commercial. An edu-mercial. A perfect example is by Orabreath Tough Cleaner.

Image from Pest Plus Website

(link address provided in Hyperlink Table at the end of the book)

1. Orabreath provides valuable information about … bad breath … in an entertaining way.
2. Orabreath sets the stage by describing what everyone wants to avoid (emotional fear) … bad breath.
3. Orabreath provides information on how to tell if YOU have bad breath in an entertaining way.
4. Afterwards, you **BUY** Orabreath's product.

A video can be a combination of styles. For example, a video resume can include a demonstration or information about upcoming trends and testimonials from previous employers or clients. An interview can include a how-to, or demonstration. Your testimonials can be in an interview format like the <u>video</u> I was asked to do (no preparation, one take) by <u>Pest Plus</u>.

In all five styles, the main character is your target audience: the person or group watching your video for their perceived need. The viewers need to see themselves in the situation you describe. Your story must invoke at least two positive emotions in your target audience in order to connect with them in a 2 to 3 minute video. Positive emotions like the ones listed in this table from <u>Self-Improvement Mentor</u>:

Adequate	Awe	Assured	Able
Capable	Certain	Charmed	Cheerful
Comfortable	Compassion	Courageous	Confidence
Determined	Delighted	Eager	Energetic
Enthusiastic	Excited	Exhilarated	Expectant
Elation	Empathy	Excellent	Fascinated
Glad	Good	Great	Grateful
Glorious	Glamorous	Graceful	Happy
Hopeful	Humorous	Inspired	Interested

Joyful	Magnificent	Lust	Love
Pleasure	Playfulness	Peaceful	Pleasant
Powerful	Pride	Positive	Relaxed
Relieved	Satisfied	Surprised	Sympathy
Stable	Sublime	Superior	Thrilled

You are the secondary character...the distributor of information. Sorry, but even if you are the expert in your field and are the best supplier of a skill, you are the secondary character. You are the voice that distributes the information to the main character...your viewer. In a movie, this role is called the "impact" or "secondary" character. Everything you do as the impact character is to support the main (your customer) character. You are the facilitator to help the main character (your customer) reach their desired goal. Your story on every video, therefore, must be in terms of your audience. It's what <u>Patricia Fripp</u> calls the I:U Ratio (the number of times you use the word "I" versus the term or reference "You" meaning to your audience).

Pat & Patricia Fripp
(link address provided in Hyperlink Table at the end of the book)

Alter-egos are allowed, sparingly. If you have a mascot your audience can relate to, it may be fun for your audience to see them in your videos. This is especially

true with pets. People LOVE their pets and spend a great deal of money on them. *Warning:* putting a pet in your video specifically to manipulate your audience's feelings will backfire. However, if you are known to have a pet and your pet has become part of your brand, go ahead and show off the paws, fins, and feathers. Even if you have eight pets! Pets add emotional appeal, as well as comic relief, between you and your audience. Just look at the <u>video</u> I created to be submitted to a <u>Daniel Pink</u> contest.

Scarlet & Pat
(link address provided in Hyperlink Table at the end of the book)

For example: I love parrots. My own parrot is on my avatar on most of the social networking sites. I was at a networking event when someone across the room shouted "Look, there's the parrot lady." It has stuck. You will see many videos featuring Scarlet, my Solomon Island Eclectus female parrot/princess. It's a trigger. When people see a parrot on TV, in a magazine, or anywhere, it has stimulated him or her to give me a call, send me (or Scarlet) an email, OR PURCHASE MY PRODUCT! It is part of my individual brand.

Know Your Audience

Times have changed. No longer is the promotion model similar to the times of TV when there was only 3 main

channels. In those days (and unfortunately still) our senses get bombarded with people talking AT us through advertisements. TiVo™ started the transformation. People now just skip over the commercials. The Internet changed the world again. With more choices to choose what to read and watch, your only avenue to reach your audience is by providing what they **feel** *(aka perceive)* is valuable. A little reinforcement may be in order:

- ► Who is going to read what you write?
- ► Who is going to watch what you produce?
- ► What do they already know?
- ► What do they want (not need) to learn?
- ► What do you want them to learn?
- ► And what do you want them to do once they are at your website?

Make sure you use language that your audience will understand, no jargon. Words which make sense to you may not mean the same thing to your readers. Think of it this way: they will search for you using *their* words—not yours!

Choose Your Tone and Words Carefully

It is the combination of emotion and information you provide in each video that determines the connection and how long viewers continue to watch. How well you combine emotion and information will determine the spreadability. Emotional connection always builds the bond before information. Your connection needs to be on

an emotional level first. This emotional connection is conveyed by facial expression and tone.

Is Your Tone Fine

Tone is heard and absorbed way before the words are heard and understood. I gave a humorous speech once titled the "Four Letter 'F' Word." Now, before you jump to conclusions...the four letter F word was FINE. Think about a gentleman answering a question from his date: "How do I look?" The responsive tone had illustrated a spark in his eye and a smile of delight.

Compare this to a response after years of answering the question when the husband doesn't even look up from the newspaper. The response was short; absent of emotion. You can imagine the wife's response.

Compare the tone to how a teenager responds to the request of the parent. The tone has emotion...a negative one probably.

Before you choose your words, practice your tone. Make sure you connect to your audience with the right tone of voice. Make sure you are conveying the right positive emotion. Lecturing turns off the ears. Parental or condescending tone turns off the ears and turns customers away. Positive, upbeat, inspirational tone provides a feeling of hope and will increase what is being heard and watched.

Are Your Words Correct

Visual words help the audiences paint a picture in their minds. You may have an image in the background of something bright and happy, but if your words conflict

with the image, your message will not be absorbed. Words that can be remembered...and stick are words that are concrete, concise, and can be put on a bumper sticker. The bumper-sticker words create the "ah-ha" moment for the viewer.

Jeffrey Gitomer & Pat
(link address provided in Hyperlink Table at the end of the book)

You want your words to make your customers think of you. The best way to achieve this is to ask powerful questions. Power questions draw in your audience. Watch this great video by Jeffrey Gitomer, a top sales training professional.

Are Your Images Compelling

TED (Technology, Entertainment and Design) is a wonderful source of sharing information. The best of the best convey their message by using the right emotional tone (urgency, empathic, inspirational), convey the information (using clear and concise examples, stories, and memorable one-liners) and images (slides). Even the most scientific of videos, can be enhanced using slides. Remember...statistics are remembered if they tell a story. Here is a great TED presentation by a master statistical

presenter, <u>Hans Rosling</u>. Learn more about creating slide presentations, check out a wonderful book by <u>Garr Reynolds</u> entitled <u>Presentation Zen</u>.

Your Objective: What Do You Want From Video

The first video is the hardest...with the second being almost as challenging. It's important to just get comfortable with videoing, editing, promoting. You can be your own worst critic. After you see the first video, you are possibly going to hate it, and begin listen to the negative feedback over those people who support your efforts. "*Ignore the nay-sayers and those who have to rain on your parade because they don't have a parade of their own*" (another great line from <u>Jeffrey Gitomer</u>). Give yourself credit for taking this step towards videography. You are doing more than most...and more than your competitors. Create up to three videos with no real business purpose in mind. After the three...it's time to get value from your time. Here are some ideas to try. Talk about what you are doing as you are videoing as a way to practice vocal variety.

- ▶ Assembling a shopping list
- ▶ What you see on a walk in the park
- ▶ Raking leaves
- ▶ Baking your special bread
- ▶ Playing cards
- ▶ Read a book out loud
- ▶ Talk to your dog, cat, parrot and kids

What Do You Want To Promote

Sure, you want to promote what you have to offer and grow your customer base. This is accomplished more by providing value with knowledge, rather than pushing your product onto the viewers. *Listen to your customer* is a common saying. For video, it is important to expand what you hear into potential ideas for your videos. For example:

1. *What are the common objections you hear from potential customers?* **List 25** of them and see how you can provide value to eliminate each objection in your video. Price or time objections tend to be smokescreens for not determining the real cause. Thinking through these objections can alert you as to whether or not you are providing the right perceived value.

2. *What difficulties do you hear about using your product or service?* What seems easy for you may not be easy for others. The word about you in the virtual community will not be good if anyone has difficulty after the purchase. Think of potential difficulties or areas that may create a misuse and potentially damage customers or your reputation. If you provide an on-site service *(physical therapy for example)*, it is common for your patient to go back home and forget how to perform the exercise. Think about instructions and demonstrations you can video that will help a customer take the action you want them to take. Videos will help someone

be hired. For example, a project manager looking for new opportunities can create a video about how to avoid scope creep or how to write a difficult review. Listen for comments from your customer. If they say they can't do something or forget, create a video. **List 10** potential trouble spots and think about how you can use video to prevent problems and facilitate greater use.

3. *What related products or services are customers also buying*? Identify what the common uses are for your product in relation to others. If you are a grocery store, show your customers how to make specific quick and easy dinners with in-season vegetables. Ask customers for their recipes (and give them credit...they will spread the word to more potential customers because their name is on the video). A realtor can interview a mortgage broker or law maintenance person. **List 10** complementary uses for your product and service in conjunction with others.

4. *Who are the experts?* Not competitors, but others who have great ideas in context of what you offer. If you sell a customer relationship management system, who are the experts your customers study about customer service, sales, and marketing? Which ones do your customers like? **List 5** people or groups (if you are local, think of at least one local person or group) you can interview or promote their views (which are the same as yours).

For example, a wedding photographer can interview a banquet hall manager.

With these lists, you have identified at least **50 content topics** for your videos. So what are you waiting for? Let start making you money by demonstrating your value through video!

How to Promote

This is the era of DIY (Do-It-Yourself). No one expects perfection...people are looking for help. What you know and share is much more important than the video quality and editing skill. So think about what your viewers would like to know or learn. Think about different ways you can share your knowledge. Make a list of **five to ten topics** which can provide that information to your viewers. Next, decide which style of video you can use to convey the information.

Let's take a look again at the five different styles of videos and how you can use them to provide perceived value.

> ► *Testimonial:* Video testimonials are great for building trust with potential customers. Potential customers see the passion existing customers feel and further illustrate that you know what you are talking about. *Gather 5 to 10 second comments* of customers talking about their perceived value, thereby eliminating what may be a common objection.

► *How To/Demonstration:* These are instructional videos for the do it yourselfers. They are related to what you have to offer without being promotional. They are educational, such as how to brine a turkey. Martha Stewart has created a real brand illustrating how to create wonderful things for the home. Some people may actually attempt creating some of them. Most of the viewers watch in awe. It doesn't matter. She built a brand as an "expert" with her *how to* knowledge. For a technician applying for a new opportunity, be careful not to overwhelm prospective employers. Demonstrate what you know by providing comfort to the prospective employer without having a know-it-all attitude. Make a **list of 5** how-to topics surrounding one aspect of what you sell.

► *Informational:* This is not a commercial. These are reviews. It is providing your personal opinion about related products and services. If you are a photographer, talk about different cameras, tripods, and flashes. You may sell these products, but that's not the goal. The goal is to help you think like your customer. Think about what viewers (consumers) are looking for in a product (ease of use) and how the product fares. Your goal is to HELP your customer and build trust. Trust leads to sales. Consider what other expertise you can offer beyond your products for a different series of videos. You can be the historian describing little known facts about your industry. Make a **list of 5** *historic trivia* about your industry.

▶ *Interviews:* It's just not guilt by association...its credibility by association. This is why it is so important to always keep your camera with you. So many experts are willing to be part of your video. After all, it helps promote their brand as well. If you bump into one of these experts on the street, ask if you can take a 1 minute video clip. Remember, luck is preparedness meeting opportunity! Have **5 questions** in your head before you ask for the interview. If you sell school products, interview teachers. Ask the teachers about what they do (not how they use your product). Share the wealth of information and increase your trust. Your viewership will be impressed because you are able to get the interview.

▶ *Promotion:* Promotional videos are more commercial-oriented. It is perfect for "product launch"; announcing a new offering to your already loyal viewers. You may be talking about the book you are selling, a special product deal, a new house that recently became available, or a new webinar. When you do create a promotional style video, the goal is to be enticing and short. Mention your "offer". Include a call to action (act now and receive 10% off your purchase). This "selling" style video should be the last style of video you implement. People will watch your promotional video **AFTER** you have earned their trust through any of the other styles of video. People are wise to know that a movie trailer shows the best part of

the movie (and may only be the best parts of the movie). Put this style video towards the end of your to-do list...after you have earned loyal followers on the web.

Each of video styles builds a community of trust. Each video style has an opening, a middle, and a closing. Each video has a goal. Each video includes a call for action as a way to GROW your community. You aren't talking AT the viewer...you are enticing them to participate. Every video needs to ask for comments on the topic of the video. Even the promotion style needs to solicit and provide comments. Think Amazon.

With all the different options and opportunities, I'm sure you are getting the sense you will be creating more than one video. Don't panic. All you need to realize is that you have multiple options. All you need to know is that you can create just one video or a series. You can grow one step at a time, one day at a time. I'll provide the tools and process to save you time and money.

Video Strategy

Video Strategy is about defining the path to build trust in you (your product or service). It's about letting people get to know you and what you value, and become part of their inner circle of trust.

Let's define your video strategy by answering the following ten questions:

1. What is your passion?
2. How does your product/service relate to your passion?
3. Who is your target audience?
4. Where does this target audience hang out online?
5. How will you know they have the same passion?
6. What objections may your target audience have to your passion (and product/service) and becoming a follower?
7. Which style of video can be used to address the target audience objections?
8. What is the knowledge you want to share with your following?
9. Which style of video can be used to share that information?
10. With whom, in your community of businesses, can you partner with or interview to leverage each other's following?

OK, you are ready to start creating at least one video. Pick one video style you feel most comfortable with doing. In most cases, it will be a "how to" style video with only you staring in the video.

Planning Checklist

Before you start to prepare for your videos, review the following checklist for completion:

- ☑ Defined clearly and concisely a definition as to my emotional "why" I'm in the business doing what I'm doing.
- ☑ Defined clearly and concisely a picture of my target audience.
- ☑ Defined and sequenced potential video projects.
- ☑ Defined the message and story for each video project.
- ☑ Defined the style of video for each video project.
- ☑ Defined the emotional triggers for each video project.
- ☑ Defined clients, colleagues and experts to interview for a video project.
- ☑ Define the goal of each video.

Scene 2: Prepare

I started talking about preparation in the previous planning section. I covered:

- Know your **why**
- Know your customer
- Know what you want to talk about
- Define a path

Your Message

Every video has a message. That message needs to relate to your "one thing", as Curly discussed in City Slickers, which gets your juices running. That "one thing" which makes four hours seems like five minutes. Each video can make one and only one point. The actual single-point message must be expressed in one concise statement. That one statement must be expressed in terms of the audience. What is the ONE point of your first video?

Where do you get ideas? Ask your customers first. They will know what they want to learn, see, or do. They will be your first source.

Your videos are about increasing sales. Look beyond your best customers to those who face a constraint which inhibits their ability to solve the problems they face in their lives. What traits does your potential customer share with your existing customer demographics? Can your product or service be stretched, altered, or modified to reach these customers? You have a lot of areas where

you can expand your reach with a tweak here or there. Think about related products and building a bridge which compliments both. A customer rarely buys what you think they are buying. The customer is buying a hammer because he or she needs to embed a nail...or connect two related or unrelated items. Cirque-du-Soleil™ is not a circus. Cirque-du-Soleil™ presents a play which attracts the theater going customer; a customer who will pay much more than going to the circus for the theater experience.

Your Structure

Every video should have an opening, closing and middle. Although, not videoed in that order. This is the order of developing your video presentation. Your opening is the most important part of the video. It is the enticement to viewer to want to watch more. The opening of your video shows the context of what the viewer will see (and learn) from your video. Your opening sets the stage for the purpose of the video and creates the desire to continue watching the video to the end.

The opening and closing should be related. Think of a circle. You are making your one point message twice. Each must be impactful. Think WIIFM (what's in it for 'me' (aka audience)). Why would the audience want to watch your video? Are you reducing a fear, supplying needed knowledge, or providing some entertainment? Phrase both the opening and the closing in terms of the audience. Don't use the word "I". "I'm going to teach you" will instantaneously have your viewer go to the

competitor's video! Phrase the statement in terms of "You". The old adage of tell 'em what you are going to tell 'em, tell 'em, and tell 'em what you told 'em completes the circle.

For example:

A bad introduction:

"I'm a commercially and self-published author of articles, chapters and books. I've written 9 separate books. This is my process."

A good introduction:

"You may think you can't get published. You may think you can but have no idea how to get started. You may actually have done it but do not know how to leverage your work. Well, if I can do it...so can YOU!"

Now, doesn't the second opening better draw the audience in? It's not about me. It's about the audience. For at least one of those three statements in the "good introduction", an audience member will be able to relate on an emotional level and want to continue watching the video. Who cares if I've written nine books (ok, maybe my 93 year old mother)? People want to know how you can help THEM. Draw them in by describing everything in terms of your number one character...your target audience of existing and POTENTIAL customers. Now, rephrase your point in terms of your audience. If possible, phrase it as a question.

The closing is just a reminder, drawing in the point, and leaving them motivated to try.

> "If someone like me who stinks at grammar can get published, so can you. Post questions you may have below. Email me when you get published!"

What's important on this closing is the encouragement that the viewer can get published. The closing reminded the customer about the opening while pulling in a reminder of a story discussed in the middle section. Closings are important. They are like the cake at the end of the wedding. A bad cake leaves a bad taste in the mouth and is remembered long after the wedding. A great cake is remembered for years (sometimes beyond the life of the marriage). Write a tasty closing which encourages your viewers to act.

If you are providing something special to your customers (how to enter a contest, a special private source to more material), you need to build the suspense and provide the information in your video. You will entice them during your opening by telling your audience what they will get at the end. At the closing, you must provide the information. This special offering is a tease or a hook to encourage the audience to watch the entire video. It is effective for videos lasting more than five minutes.

The other important nuance is the call to action. Viewers will be caught up in your video. They are not thinking about giving feedback. Feedback (via a comment, a "subscribe" and a "like") is the holy grail of social media.

The more comments, subscriptions, and likes raise your chances of appearing first on search engines (like Google). Snowball had over 4 million views. His dance steps also received over 5,000 comments and 10,000 likes. All of which, according to Irena, director of BirdLoversOnly.org, lead Snowball's video to create a funnel for money *to start coming in like water!*

The middle of the video can have up to three points, sub-sections, of your message. People think along linear lines. Each sub-point should be stated in a logical order. Don't lose your audience by rambling out of sequence. Help them by transitioning from point-to-point in a logical order. Don't lecture, have a conversation. Imagine yourself sitting at a coffee shop across from a close friend. Write down your three points.

The smoother the transition between the points, the better your audience will be able to follow you. What may seem logical for you as the next step may be an abrupt and startling change in topics to the novice viewer. Think of a sentence you can use to transition from one point to the other. A form of a bookend to your thoughts.

You can add a transition at the beginning by stating "It takes three steps to get out this stain." ... "Step one" ... "step two" ... "step three" ... "We have completed the three steps to removing your stain." Even if you use transitional slides, a verbal clue you are changing topics will improve the experience for your viewers.

Think and write down how you will transition between your topics. The terms must be related (as in the word "step") to keep the continuity throughout your video.

Video Is About Imagery Too

A video is more like a movie than a keynote presentation or instructional class. You have options. A speech full of talk is not as interesting as a video with imagery. As in the movies, much of what is conveyed is through non-verbal communication. For example: Standing in front of a beautiful, slightly populated beach will convey the tranquility of the beach-property you are selling. Showing the consistency of the dough is more powerful than trying to describe it in words alone.

When you are looking at the three points you wish to convey in your video, think about how you may be able to demonstrate your point through imagery. Movies convey about 50% of the information through visual action.

The Three Act Play

Videos are the combination of a good speech and a good screenplay. Both have a beginning, middle and an end. Both are like a three act play. Based upon <u>Linda Segers</u> screenplay structure, you can see the correlation you will follow for your videos.

	Speech	**Screenplay**
ACT	Opening	Setup
ONE	Transition	First Turning Point
ACT TWO	Three Points	Story Development Action with increasing levels of chaos/obstacles to be surmounted (similar to points)
	Point or Step 1	
	Point 1 -> 2 Transition	
	Point or Step 2	
	Point 2 -> 3 Transition	
	Point or Step 3	
ACT	Transition	Second Turning Point
THREE	Closing	Resolution

Your timing is the same as well. Act 2 takes ½ of your video time. The remaining half is split between Act 1 and Act 3. For example: A 3 minute video is made up of 180 seconds. Dividing the 180 seconds in half equates to the 90 (or 1.5 minutes) for the meat of your video. The opening and closing will be 45 seconds each. Not a lot of time.

Within the Act One's 45 seconds, you will need to dedicate time for your:

- ▶ Title slide,
- ▶ Opening to set the stage
- ▶ A tease (hook) of anything special provided AT THE END of the video, and
- ▶ Transition to Act 2.

Within the Act Three's 45 seconds, you will need to dedicate time for your:

- ► Transition from Act 2,
- ► Summary statement,
- ► Give them what you promised in the beginning of the video,
- ► The hook (if this video is part of a series...what will come next),
- ► Explain what is available FREE and HELPFUL on your website,
- ► Call to action, and
- ► Company information slide.

The table that follows provides some guidelines for your video. Keep in mind that shorter videos are watched and shared more. Longer videos are good for how-to and training among specific followers (aka customers). It is recommended to keep your opening and closing under 5 minutes, even for longer presentations.

	ACT ONE	**ACT TWO**	**ACT THREE**
2 Minute Video	30 seconds	1 minute (make 1 point only)	30 seconds
3 Minute Video	45 seconds	1-1/2 minutes (make 1 point only)	45 seconds
7 Minute Video	1-1/2 minutes	4 minutes (make up to 3 points)	1-1/2 minutes
18 Minute Video	4-1/2 minutes	9 minutes (make 3 points)	4-1/2 minutes
30 Minute Video	5 minutes	20 minutes (make 3 points with 3 sub-points for each point)	5 minutes
45 Minute Video	5 minutes	35 minutes (make 3 points with 3 sub-points for each point)	5 minutes

Act 2 is the "action" or movement of the video to the video's conclusion or main point. This is accomplished by having three sub-points. Each sub-point needs to have a goal. Each sub-point must relate to the main point and goal of the video. Each sub-point's goal must lead (the action of the video) the viewer to the conclusion and the main purpose for the viewer to watch your video.

Write It Down

Every video should have a script with an opening, closing, and middle. It's not acted out like a movie or TV show. It's just organized that way. Memorized speeches **never** connect with an audience. Professional speakers look at the camera and never read from a script. Instead, memorize your opening statement and your closing statement. You are creating a start and end point to relieve any nervousness you might have talking to the camera. Next, remember what three points (I'll discuss tips to help you remember later in this book) you want to make and in what order. You will look and sound much more conversational and connect better with your audience. If you are going to create a series, make only ONE point, topic, or purpose for each video.

A common misconception about public speaking is you need to provide voice to the written word. Actually, that is the worst thing you can do. The best public speakers have a CONVERSATION with the audience. They know what information they want to cover and talk WITH the audience...not talk TO them.

Stories Are Remembered

A successful screenplay tells a story with memorable characters, scenes (with dialog), and events. An audience can picture your video long after the words are forgotten. A great mystery or crime is hinted to in the beginning and resolved during the climax.

- ▶ Can you share a relevant story about the three points you are providing?
- ▶ Can you tell the time when your customer brought in their "lucky" shirt full of tomato sauce stain? How did you get it out? What was the reaction from the customer?
- ▶ Can you set the scene with a mystery? Think about a short story which illustrates your points. If you can, express the story like a screenplay by using dialog. "Jim rushed into the dry cleaners shouting. 'My lucky baseball shirt is ruined. I have a big game tomorrow. How can I possibly win without wearing my lucky baseball shirt?'" Be expressive with the character, scene and event. Use vivid descriptions so the audience can *feel* and *visualize* they were there.

Ask For Participation

Social media is about the conversation within a community. The community includes those loyal to you for what you do, purchasers (who may not become loyal), potential customers, and those who disagree. Allow the discussions to occur between all of them. Your structure

and content needs to provide an avenue that you create for the conversation. This won't occur without a *call of action* by you asking for their thoughts. It's not just telling them to leave a comment at the *end*. It's about *starting* the conversation by asking for their thoughts, ideas, and opinions whenever possible. Make sure the question relates to your topic. For example, "What is your favorite pasta dish?" is a good question for a video discussing different tomatoes or Italian ingredients.

Think about questions you can ask to encourage a response left in the comment section on your YouTube channel, blog, or Facebook. Encourage involvement. Encourage the building of a "tribe" or community for your topic. Proactively call your loyal following to illustrate that he or she has the same passion as you.

Some examples:

1. How did your kids like this recipe? What did you do to change the recipe that you found to make it taste even better?

2. What is the working title of the book you are working on with me during this series? State your commitment by adding your working title in the comment section.

3. Was this tip useful for you? Do you have any other related tips? Share it with this community by adding a comment below.

4. Which is your favorite restaurant near this senior community? What tips do you have about what to order?

5. What information would you like to see in future videos? We want to provide this service to you.

Use the language of your target audience. Use words the audience will understand immediately. This includes slang words, technical acronyms, and informal expressions. You want your call to action to trigger the action; not make your viewer spend time thinking about what you are trying to say.

Prepare Checklist

Now for a quick checklist on how to prepare for your videos before the next practice section.

- ☑ What is your customers' main reason for watching your video?
- ☑ How will you open your video? What questions will you ask in terms of your viewership?
- ☑ Will your opening provide a quick grasp by your viewers as to what is in it for them?
- ☑ How will you close your video? What statement will or can inspire your viewer to act on what is discussed?
- ☑ Does the opening and closing complement each other?
- ☑ Does the opening and closing take valuable time away from the middle?
- ☑ What three sub-points in relation to your main point you will cover in your video? In what order will you cover them?
- ☑ What stories (with dialog if possible) can you include to emphasize a point?
- ☑ How will you transition between the main and sub-points of the video?
- ☑ How can you add to your message with imagery?
- ☑ What "call to action" will you encourage your viewers to take to encourage participation and community development?

Scene 3: Practice

You do NOT need to be a professional speaker to be credible and inspiring in your video. What you need to use are a few tips to keep connected to your audience. These few tips will separate you from the amateur. These simple to use tips come from experts like <u>Patricia Fripp</u> *(a professional speaker for all reasons)*, <u>Garr Reynolds</u> *(Presentation Zen),* and the tried and true <u>Toastmasters Organization</u> *(the best kept secret to getting comfortable*

Seth Godin & Pat
(link address provided in Hyperlink Table at the end of the book)

in front of anyone...including a camera). These are tips used by master speakers like <u>Jeffrey Gitomer</u> *(sales),* <u>Seth Godin</u> *(marketing),* and <u>Les Brown</u> *(motivation).* All three have a very different style. All three convey their messages in short inspiring videos using the techniques described in *Your Video Playbook.*

Remember that old saying? *How do you get to Carnegie Hall? Practice! Practice! Practice!* Perfection on video is less important than content. However, practice will make you feel more comfortable and give you a leg up on your competition. Let's incorporate these tips into your practice session.

- *Filler Words:*   Ah, um, you know, without further ado, ok and the power of pauses.
- *Think About It:*   Energy, speed, and eye contact draws your audience to you.
- *Variety:*   Dress, appropriate hand gestures and vocals.

Practice these tips during your everyday interaction with people. As you improve, you will notice they will all become more involved in what you have to say. This will also happen on video.

The Need for Silence

People rarely think about what you said while you are talking. Pauses (count s l o w l y from 1 to 3) allow your audience an opportunity to turn off their listening and absorb the point you are making. Therefore, you are not really getting your message out if you talk non-stop.

This is the problem with filler words. The um's, ah's, you know, OK, all right, and all those other words you don't even think you are saying but do. These are "filler" words. These filler words take away the valuable seconds of silence your audience needs to absorb your message. The words do not add any value to your message. They fill the space that should be silent (again, count slowly from 1 to 3). Without realizing it, you are losing credibility with every filler word you say on your video. One or two may creep in. Everyone has a slip or two. The point is to

replace the "you know" habit with what will help you make more sales...silence...think time for your viewers.

Use all your time to begin to eliminate filler words from your conversations. Practice talking all the time without them. Ask a friend, coworker, or family member to secretly count the number of filler words you used during a conversation. It will take time, but you will improve and your videos will be better for it. You need to allow silence for the audience to stop listening and tell his or her brain to absorb and think about what you just said.

The other problem with speaking in videos is the run-on sentence. I've heard people combine thoughts with the word "and". A person might be talking for 3 minutes and never take a breath, and it will be one sentence because they used the word "and", eliminating silent pause opportunities. Only use the word "and" if you are providing a list. "You can add the cake flour and regular flour during this step." The word "AND" should never be used more than once in a sentence or breath.

Connect With Energy

The goal of every video is to connect with each viewer as if you are talking only to him or her. Begin by talking to the camera, looking at the camera as if you are speaking directly to that one person. The camera light is the eye of your viewer. Think of the light as your best friend, favorite customer, loved-one, child, or beloved pet...anyone you are happy (passionate) to be talking to

about this topic. Your attention and speech should be to whom you speak directly on a one-on-one basis.

People connect better with friendly people. A smile illustrates that you are friendly and approachable. Remember to display the appropriate level of smile (serious discussions can still have the occasional small smile of comfort).

Tone is heard and absorbed before words are understood. Sound friendly, not arrogant. No one relates to a know-it-all. Everyone relates to someone who sounds like he or she is open and want to be helpful. Avoid words which give a negative tone such as "well", "if it were me", "should". You may be the expert but people are turned off by "know- it-alls". Why?...Because "know-it-alls" don't!

Your audience will adjust to your energy level. If you want calm, relaxed viewers...be relaxed. If you want people to be excited, sound excited. That doesn't mean you need to be excited throughout the entire video. Variety is extremely important. The variety in energy level adds interest. You don't want to be the "Billy Mays" professional TV direct-response pitchman for your videos. You want to open up with a middle level of energy and move your audience to the level you want (up or down). If you want your audience to be highly energized and you begin highly energized, you have nowhere to go but down.

Stand up when possible. You sound more energetic standing up. Sitting down in a chair is fine, if you remain

energetic. Slouching at all will portray lack of self-esteem. A swinging chair exemplifies your nervousness.

SLOW DOWN! The <u>FedEx commercial with fast talking people</u> was funny. No one, however, remembers what he said. You want people to remember your valuable message. Video aren't a commercial. They are a one-to-one relationship builder. Not everyone is a Wall Street trader who listens with that speed or intensity.

Remember...watch your tone.

Variety Is the Spice of Life

Vocal variety (in pitch, volume and tone) keeps the audience interest. Monotone vocals put people to sleep. Just as with the energy level, vocals need to adjust throughout each video to keep the audience's attention. Look for opportunities to add reflection into your script.

Variety applies to sentence structure as well. Ensure that your sentences vary in length and structure. The same length sentence (or syllable count) throughout your video creates a see-saw affect. This affect also lulls people to sleep.

Hand gestures draw in the audience. You will be videoing yourself from the waist up. Keep your arms at your side. Occasionally use them to motion people to you or to them (in both directions). Use hand movements only when it adds to your content and topic. You don't want to look like a bird ready to take flight. You can point down when

asking for their participation by leaving a comment or liking or sharing your video. Use your hands to enhance your topic or point. Hand movements add "imagery" to your video.

Facial expressions are also important. If you are passionate about your topic, your eyes need to show your passion. If you are happy, look happy. If you are talking about something serious, show it in your facial muscles. Think and watch news anchors. Imagery is absorbed before tone and words. Have 50% of your video convey your message through images.

You don't have to wear a suit if your audience is not a corporate 50 company. Wear the clothes appropriate to your topic. If you are talking about sports, wear a team shirt. If you are baking, wear an apron. Whatever you wear, make sure you are clean and presentable. Make sure it fits. Too big or too tight clothing distracts from your message and portrays a message of cheap and sloppy. Even t-shirts (with your company logo) require ironing. Any wrinkles will create shadows which are magnified on video. This is your image we are talking about. If you have a company shirt, wear it to reinforce your brand. If you can, use a different color once in a while. Variety is the spice of life.

Encourage responses to your videos. Pull in your customer related videos onto your channel via a playlist (more about playlist and channel set up later in this book). As an example, Toyota pulled in videos of those

who parodied their <u>swagger wagon video</u> to create a series around a community of followers.

The Bond with the Trusted Advisor

Your goal with every video is to build a level of trust with your audience. This is accomplished by being authentic; not a movie or TV star. Successful videos are those who show the face of the company. It is not a TV commercial. Show you are a real person.

You will know you have a bond with your audience by how they participate with you by:

► Opt-in to your email list (the golden ring)
► Subscribing to your video channel.
► Click through to your website.
► Connecting through your social media presence.
► Spreading the word about your video.

YouTube is not the best place to sell. YouTube is THE place to earn and maintain trust with customers (existing and potential). Use YouTube to become their trusted advisor and drive them back to your website. Give your customers what they want on YouTube. Once they go to your site, you can give them what they need. A need doesn't mean a market...until you earned their trust.

Practice Checklist

Let's review what needs to be remembered as you practice for your videos.

- ☑ What filler words do I use and need to remove from my conversation? Who can help me remove them?
- ☑ What outfits can I wear for different videos while maintaining to my brand?
- ☑ What energy can I add and when should it be added to create the right mood by the viewer?
- ☑ Where can I add pauses to the conversation to make sure my point is heard and absorbed by the viewer?

Scene 4: Present

Before you can be the star I know you are, you need to have the right location to perform. You can be in the kitchen, outside, or in your office or store. Where you are doesn't matter. As we discussed in the previous section, variety increases the attention span of your viewers. However, you do need to be careful to avoid potential distractions. You want to make sure the audience is focused on you and your message. You don't want the viewer to be thinking, "Why is he talking about spring vegetables with Christmas decorations in the background?"

Here are the key steps in presenting your message.

- ▶ *The Setup*
- ▶ *The Environment*
- ▶ *The Take*

The Setup

**Get Seen by
Steve Garfield**
(link address
provided in
Hyperlink Table at
the end of the book)

The setup refers to all the equipment you will need to make your videos. New equipment is introduced into the market daily. The videographer I like to watch to keep up with the latest and greatest video-related hardware/software is Steve Garfield. He tweets (constantly), video blogs, posts status on his Facebook page comparing products or providing his take about individual products. I strongly recommend reading his book Get Seen.

Equipment (Hardware)

You can go crazy buying all the different hardware and software to create videos. The cost can be minimal or astronomical. In the beginning, go with what you have. Your video toolbox will increase over time. As you get comfortable, you can buy the next step up or add to your collection. There are some great books that discuss different equipment for video. You can find many video reviews as new products come on the market. We list many links at the end of this book. For other options...just Google it.

► ***Camera:*** You need something with which to shoot the video. You can use your mobile phone (iPhone), a point-n-shoot (Cannon/Nikon) digital camera, a mini-video recorder (Kodak) or graduate to a cinema quality camera. It's important to start with what you own...then move up slowly. Your message is more important than the type of camera you use.

As you improve, you may want to graduate to a two- or three- camera shoot. Align the camera at different points. Keep each camera out of view of the others. Have them all "film" you from different perspectives. From the right side, direct, and left. You may also decide on different lenses to add affect (wide-angle or fish eye). More about camera placement will be covered in a later section.

A few words about webcams: Your PC may already have a webcam built in. If not, you can buy one to connect to your personal computer. Personally, I'm not a fan of using webcams. People tend to look washed out, disproportion, and nervous (the chair is always swaying back and forth). People have a lower energy level that just doesn't connect well. Webcams are great for <u>Webex</u>, <u>GoToMeeting</u>, <u>Skype</u>, or webinars. For demonstrating your value- -sorry--it misses the mark (IMHO: in my humble opinion).

► **Tripod:** With that in mind, the other VERY important piece of hardware you need is a tripod. No one is steady enough to hold a camera still for a 3 minute video. Buy one with extendable legs and one good for a table top.

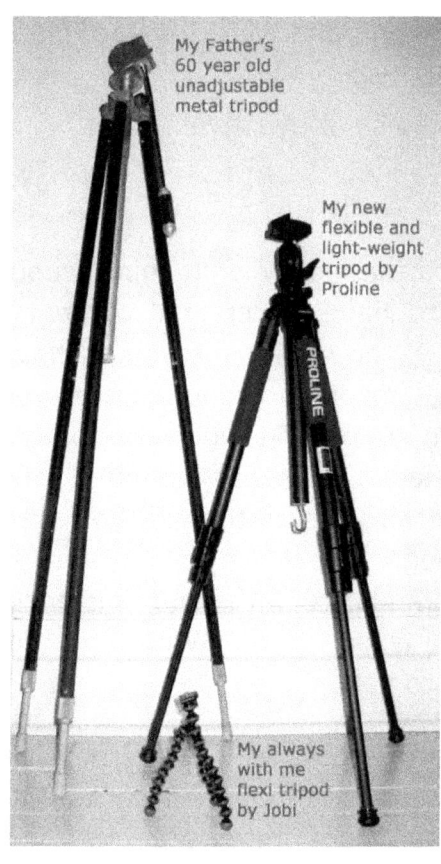

My Father's 60 year old unadjustable metal tripod

My new flexible and light-weight tripod by Proline

My always with me flexi tripod by Jobi

I actually still have my father's (a great hobby photographer) tripod. It doesn't extend and is made of heavy metal. I use it in the house only because of sentimental reasons. I have an extendable tripod I take with me when I know I'm going to shoot video. I purchased the one that extends above 5 feet to make sure I have a better chance to take the video at eye level.

I have a flexi-table top tripod that is only 6" long. It fits well in my purse so I have it with me ALL THE TIME. The flexible legs allow me to wrap the tripod around anything stable ... even a stop sign. It's great for those moments of brilliance when an idea for a video comes to mind or I bump into someone I would love to interview. Here is a <u>video</u> I made to illustrate where people can find 15

15 Minute Spoof on YouTube
(link address provided in Hyperlink Table at the end of the book)

minutes to work on writing a book (also applies to creating a video).

If you do not have a tripod when you have an idea for a video, don't wait. Instead, place the video recorder on a flat service at eye level.

▶ ***Computer:*** Just in case you didn't think about it...it's a good idea to have a personal computer (laptop or desktop; PC or Apple) for you to have control of your social media presence. Sure, you can hire someone to do all the work. In today's environment, you need a personal computer and access to the Internet. Your smartphone, however, may have good enough access for you to answer questions or to communicate with your audience. Which brand you use is up to you. Which Internet service access, is up to you.

The camera, tripod and access to the Internet (via a smartphone or PC) are the three *must haves*. The other nice-to-have hardware items are tools you can build upon after you take AND POST (which is the objective) a few videos.

► ***Lighting:*** Lighting is extremely important in making good videos. You may be able to use what Mother Nature has provided or what modern humans have invented for in home use. You can even buy specific lighting equipment when you build or rent your video studio. In all cases, you are looking to have the lighting improve how you look. You do not want to look washed out or like you are telling a ghost story around the camp fire on a camping trip (unless this is your intent...Halloween-themed video). You want to look natural. Whatever lighting you use, have the light behind the camera shining on you. For natural sunlight, watch out for clouds.

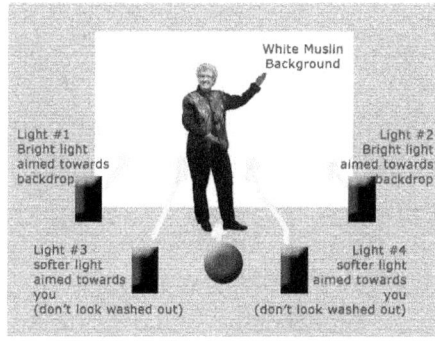

If you are using a professional "studio" setup, use a white background with three or four professional florescent lights. Two of the lights aimed towards the backdrop to make the background look as white and bright as possible. One or two lights are aimed towards you. Your camera, on a tripod, is aimed towards you. Make sure the lights are outside of the camera view.

In my first testimonial I found what would have been a beautiful background for a photograph (a

common mistake). The sky was overcast. The start of the testimonial looked great...after 10 seconds, the sun went in and out of the clouds creating over-exposed and under-exposed faces. Don't think like a photographer, think like a moviemaker. When inside, turn on all the lights, keep windows behind the camera, not behind the subject. When outside, be ready to take several takes if the environment is changing the lighting effects.

Never let the viewer see you sweat! If it's hot outside, drink a cold glass of water before your speak. Put on a little powder (you too men) to absorb any potential sweat on your forehead. If you are shooting from the waist up, wear darker clothes to prevent underarm sweat marks from glistening in the sunlight.

► ***Sound:*** Sound equipment is the next important tool. The mini video recorders require you to be

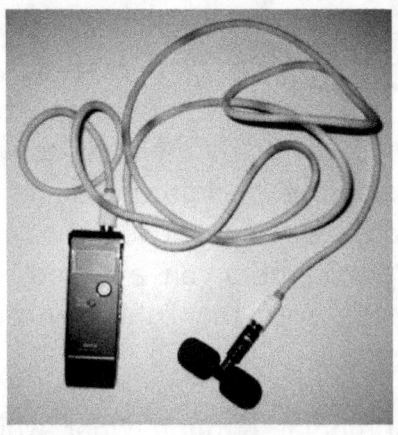

within 3 feet of the subject to get the best sound. I purchased the Kodak Zi8 in 2010 because it allowed an external microphone. As a professional speaker, I already had a stereo

Lavaliere microphone that fit perfectly. However, I still didn't like the sound. Now I can set the camera up about five feet from the subject. I place my mini Sony audio recorder with a small stereo microphone. I attach it to the back pocket of the person I'm videoing. It is easy enough to sync the audio with the video with today's available software. I actually do this manually. It is very easy. Visit <u>Steve Garfield's</u> site for different great reviews of equipment and software.

▶ ***AudioRecorder:*** Digital audio devices have come down in price. For under $100 you can purchase one even a reporter uses (Sony/Olympus) or a four channel version (zoom). The more channels, the more flexibility you will have to remove background noise from your video.

▶ ***Storage:*** A BIG warning. Videos take up **a lot** of space on your PC, especially if you are taking them in High Definition. You may want to consider buying a separate terabyte drive to store your videos. I grew up in the Information Technology world. When I first started in the late 1970's, PC's weren't even invented yet. What took up an entire floor of specially cooled space now fits in a 4"x6"x1/2" drive. What used to cost millions of dollars, today you can buy for less than $100! BUY EXTRA STORAGE!

▶ ***Props:*** Other equipment you should think about are props. Use props sparingly. If it isn't directly

Enterprise Architecture Explanation
(link address provided in Hyperlink Table
at the end of the book)

related to what you are discussing, leave it out. If your prop promotes your brand, keep it in the background. If you are an author, have the book you are promoting either in your hand (read a paragraph or two) or in the background. If you are selling a service, have a mug with your logo in the background as I did in the M&M Enterprise Architecture video. If you sell bagels, have bagels on display somewhere in the video shot. Remember, imagery conveys 50% of your message. If you will be handling a prop, practice picking it up and showing it while you are looking and talking to a camera (or kids, dog, cat, parrot).

Equipment (Software)

Your camera may come with its own video editing software. Your computer may have come with video editing software. Some video players have software. YouTube offers basic editing software as well. If none of these options have what you need, there are many products available for your PC or Apple computer. What's important is not all the bells and whistles but what you feel comfortable in using and whether or not your computer has enough memory to run the program. Some software programs perform only the basics. Others allow for complex special effects. Just as you grow with your hardware, you can grow with your software. It is not uncommon for you to use multiple different software products to accomplish all the "special effects" you require in varying degrees.

Make sure the software you select can support the camera's video file format at the quality level you are using. For example, not all software can support or read and edit the 1080p format now available on most cameras. This means you will need to take the video at a lower resolution like 720p to sue that software.

> ▶ ***Ease of Use:*** You can easily figure out how to use the program and the basic bells and whistles you want. I'm a big believer in making it so easy even a five year old has a good user experience with the software! As my sister used to say to help-desk operators, "Explain to me how to use this as you would explain this to your well-beloved

grandmother." That means the documentation needs to be crystal clear for non-techies to be able to use it WITHOUT A PHONE CALL to technical support.

▶ ***Capture/Playback:*** Some software allows you to capture PC window action directly into your PC, incorporating other software such as PowerPoint. For example, you can tell the software to "record" as you click through a slide presentation. Another example would be where the editing software allows you to "record" as you move your cursor through some other program (pulling down menu's, pointing to the save button, entering text, etc.).

▶ ***Editing:*** You can cut and move around parts of one or more videos to create one video. Not all software allows you to change the lighting affect.

▶ ***Effects/Transitions:*** Adding title slides, animation (some even 3D) and other transitional effects adds a level of professionalism to your video. As with props, don't overdo.

▶ ***Audio and Photo Editing:*** Pick software which allows you to at least add audio and photographs for background or picture in picture affects. Some software of the more advanced products allow you to create your own audio and photo editing in the same product. Some provide you with a "green screen" replacement where you can change the

background image like the movie and TV studios use.

▶ ***Audio to Text:*** Some software allows for the ability to translate the audio voice to text. This is great for closed caption. If the translation can be exported, even better. Google is the number one search engine...they do their search on text, not video or audio. Having your video appear on your blog post ALONG with the translated text, increases your "Google Juice". If your software does not allow you to convert audio to text, see if you can export just the audio portion of the video. There are software packages that can translate audio files.

▶ ***Linkable Text:*** YouTube provides some editing software. They also provide "annotations" where you can add text that is clickable (currently only to another YouTube function—unless you are a not-for-profit organization) from the video. The text appears when you want it to appear. This is great if you have a series and you can tell the viewer to click to view the next in the series, previous in the series, or SUBSCRIBE TO YOUR CHANNEL (the best of the annotation "note" functions).

▶ ***Export/Production:*** You will need to export your video. Some software allows you to upload directly to Facebook or YouTube. Some allow you to create a DVD (which is great for speakers wanting to sell their 45 minute keynote).

Your Environment

Your environment is anything within view and hearing of the video and audio recorder. Since you are promoting you, most of the footage will be with you in the viewfinder. Unless you are using a microphone, make sure you are within distance of what your camera considers good sound (usually less than 3 feet for mini-video recorders). This is especially important if you are videoing an event of some type. Your ears are much better than your camera's. Stand as close as possible to what you want to video to obtain the best audio (less than 3 feet).

If you are outside the view (for example you are taping an event), you are performing as the videographer. Don't talk. The sound level will be out of sync of what you are videoing. You can always add voice overs or turn down annoying background noises (i.e. an ambulance passing by) when you are editing. The time saver is to keep in mind you must create a good sound environment so you don't have to edit it out later.

Inside View

Before you record (even if this is an interview), spin slowly around to see what's in sight of the camera's viewpoint. Is there a spider crawling up the wall? Is the calendar year in view (not a good idea if you want your video to be useful for a decade)? Any private information within view (your bank statement) you don't care to share with the world? Are you talking about healthy-

eating with a bag of potato chips in the background? Is your office a mess presenting a sloppy image of your work? Bottom line, keep out of shot what isn't relevant or even damaging to the point you want to make.

You can be subtle with branding, place a cup with your company logo on the table next to you. The same is true with your published works and awards. You can zoom in and out so the brand isn't in view all the time. Start and end with these "extras" in sight. Zoom in when you need your viewers to concentrate on your message. Zoom out before you end your speech.

Stand away from walls to enhance the look of the video. When you stand next to a wall, you lose depth of field and "character" to the "footage". Your video will look flat and be less appealing to the viewer's eye. Imagery is important!

What are you wearing? Granted, what you are wearing may not always be an option. You might find a video moment and you didn't plan your outfit. You have a stain on your shirt from painting, but the final product is exactly what you wanted to convey to your audience. Don't let the video moment pass. Take the video and see what actually shows up. But...if you can plan ahead, plan your wardrobe as well. Solid outfits rather than printed outfits blend better with the environment.

Get Published!
Video Series

By Pat Ferdinandi,
Published Author,
Speaker, & Mentor

PatF@SBDi-Consulting.com
More info: squidoo.com/get-published

Scarlet & my published works
Episode 1
(link address provided in Hyperlink Table at the end of the book)

When I made my first video series, "Get Published," I wanted to be in the room where I had a wall hanging of the cover of one of my books. The wallpaper was very busy and clashed terribly with the printed jacket I was wearing. Luckily my content and enthusiasm was great. Imagine how much better my video would have been if I just wore a different outfit.

Don't let the environment be a distraction from your message.

Your Stage

In most cases, you will be videoing yourself in a single location. You can sit in a chair or in front of your computer. Sit anywhere you feel comfortable and calm and calmness will be what comes across in your video. You do not want to sway in a chair, twirl your hair, play with the change in your pocket, or tap your hands on a pen, table or lecture.

When I gave my first presentation for "Get Published," I wanted to make sure I made eye-contact with different

audience members. I walked from one side of the room to the other. I had only one camera with me. I had set up the camera to focus on me standing in one spot. For giving a speech, I should have remembered I have happy feet to keep different sides of the audience within eye-contact. Unfortunately, I kept on walking off camera. I should have moved the camera back a foot to get a wider view or used a wide angle lens. I could have used multiple cameras placed so I would be in view of at least one camera.

Remember the movie "*Awakenings*" with Robert DeNiro and Robin Williams? Robin Williams, playing a doctor, noticed that when a change in the floor pattern occurred, the patient (Robert DeNiro) wouldn't cross it. Well, this occurs with us as well.

I want to stand and talk. My energy level is higher. Unfortunately, I have happy feet whenever I stand. I finally took out my Halloween floor mat. I placed it where I wanted to stand for my video. Subconsciously, I NEVER took a step off the mat. I couldn't believe it...so I tested it with others. I attended a <u>Toastmasters</u> meeting and insisted everyone use the mat for their 1 minute, 2

minute, and 10 minute talk. NO ONE! I mean NO ONE stepped off the mat. I mean even those who had worse happy feet than I have (which is significant) stayed in place. Even newbies who were so nervous giving their first speech stayed on the Halloween floor mat. I'm talking about experienced stand-up comedians. <u>Happy Feet</u> may have been a great movie, but it's not good for the video recorder. The speakers were like the patients in Awakenings. They did not cross the "line".

If your stage requires panning, where you are walking with the camera between two points, WALK S L O W L Y ! You want a smooth transition. Changing scenery every second or two creates a restless feeling for the viewer. You want to make your viewer's experience as pleasant as possible. Think twice about whether you need the entire walk in the shoot. You may want to keep the audio and add a slide of an image instead. You may wish to transition from the 5 seconds "let's look over here" to the final spot "and here we are". Think how bakers suddenly display a baked cake only a second after putting the batter into the oven. You only have a short time to keep the attention of any viewer. Make sure you include only what your viewer needs to see and hear. Ask yourself (while presenting and editing), what's the perceived value to the viewer.

Photographers learn about setting up a picture. Though I've learned that picture taking is very different from videoing, the principle of thirds is important. If you split your stage view into thirds, creating a tic-tac-toe board, you want to place yourself at one of the cross points. You

do not always want to be smack in the center. Though Jeffrey Gitomer does this effectively with a solid white background, for the novice, it will be better to zoom in and create the tic-tac-toe effect. You do not want to take up the entire view. This also allows for space to add text when editing (more about "callouts" when we talk about editing).

If you are videoing outdoors, allow the sunlight to be behind the camera...not behind you. In fact, it is better that you are in the shade (but not shadows). Make sure you are representing yourself and your brand (not someone else...or a competitor). Pick a clean area like your storefront or an area that relates to your brand (a sports field to talk about sports medicine or stretching exercises).

As audio is so important, check your surroundings. If you are on a busy street or at an event, you will have a great deal of background noise. Using a lapel microphone with a separate audio device may be helpful. An audio recorder with multiple channels will allow you to eliminate some of the background noise. Better yet, pick a spot with minimal background noise. This will save you considerable time during editing.

Here is an impromptu interview I did with the copywriter, Jodi Kaplan. We were on a very busy street in New York City, New York. We had people walking in front of us chatting about a personal situation. We had people stop and look at the camera. The small cheap tripod I had at the time (it actually broke when I tried to collapse it after

the interview) could not extend so we were not at eye level but a "look up into my nose" level. We had buses, lighting problems, audio problems … but … it had important information that keeps people viewing. Heck, it added some levity to my first video. Would I do it differently if I redid this video today? Absolutely! BUT…if I didn't make the mistakes this time, I wouldn't know or understand how to improve. So…JUST DO IT! Jodi Kaplan and I had fun creating this video…and so will you.

Jodi Kaplan of KaplanCopy & Me
(link address provided in Hyperlink Table
at the end of the book)

Outside View

What's not in view of the camera can be to your benefit. If you want to make sure you cover all the important points, take a piece of flip-chart paper and write down your outline in the order you want to talk about them. Use VERY LARGE print to avoid any potential squinting to

read on your part. Place the chart next to the camera at eye level. You don't want to be looking down at the list. You want to always look straight at the camera. You also don't want your notes to be seen by the camera.

If you don't want to use cue cards or you still break your eye contact, attach a little birdie to the camera as a subconscious reminder. For those clients who are nervous, I attach a paper puppet from Campuppet. Not only does it keep the client looking at the camera, the client remains smiling.

The Take

If you are videoing yourself, practice once or twice in front of the camera. Practice looking at the right place and pulling in props at the right time without stepping out of camera view. Sure, you can edit mishaps out of the video. It just makes good sense to practice in the environment. Think of it as a dress rehearsal.

Be prepared to take more than one video. The lighting may change, you may forget what you wanted to say or flub your words. The audio may sound hollow like you are in a tunnel or you turn away from the microphone as you are talking. It happens. If you're videoing someone, warn the person it may take 2 or 3 takes. It calms your

interviewee. He or she doesn't worry about perfection and will look calmer on the takes.

Never throw away any of your takes. You may find something of value you can pull into the video you are working on or one in the future. You may only need that 5 second explanation of a complex topic you did brilliantly once. Editing is the process of piecing together the parts. You can keep a great audio and add images or screenshots (great for how-to type videos). Or you can retake the audio and add it to a close up video (where the focus isn't on your mouth but on what you are doing).

Once you video three takes (if you need that many), STOP. You are looking for perfection. If it's 75% good enough, you can use what footage you took. Otherwise, you will be stuck taking hundreds where none of them are good enough. That's when your internal fear is taking over common sense. Calm down. You'll do just fine! This is why we have used many of our not-so-good video examples throughout this book.

You don't have to be in your video all the time. Variety is the spice that increases interest. As long as you have some consistency (topic, flow, music) you are building your brand with video.

The Look

You look marvelous! You will especially look good if you are wearing something comfortable. Clean...but comfortable. If you have a company outfit, wear it! You

want all your videos to support your brand. Avoid colors which don't do well on video's, like solid red or green (more important if you have a green screen). Avoid crazy patterns which will blur or look dizzy to the viewer as you move. A mistake I have made in the past is to wear shiny jackets. In many cases, the lighting will create a glare which distracts the viewers. Another oops was discovering how wrinkles (in clothes) show up on camera, especially cotton T's or pullovers. Prepare...press your clothes before videoing.

Video Styles

As mentioned previously, I group video into five separate style categories. Let's talk about presentation format for each style:

▶ *Testimonials:* A testimonial is an impromptu event. To ask a customer to come back and provide a testimonial a day or two (or longer) later diminishes the emotional impact the customer will express on video. You really want to ask for a video testimonial at the moment a customer expresses his or her pleasure (and answers a possible objection a prospective customer may have in doing business with you). This requires preparation on your part. Go back to the exercises where you listed the potential objections a prospective customer has expressed. Always have your video taking device (iPhone, micro-video-recorder) fully charged and with you at all times.

Always ask for permission and always have them sign a release form. I have a sample form at the end of this book. Keep each take of a customer under one minute. Explain that you may only use 10 to 20 seconds of what you take. Let your customer know you may need to take up to three different takes. Give them an option of approving the final edit.

My Le Sportsac bag
(link address provided in Hyperlink Table at the end of the book)

Prepare for testimonials. You've already identified the key objections you hear from those not wanting to buy your product or service. Listen for any comment from a customer which addresses one objection and ask them to do a video testimonial. You already know what makes you different from the competition. If you hear a customer say this was the buying reason, ask for a video testimonial.

When I attended <u>Jeffrey Gitomer's</u> sales boot camp in 2007, he asked for testimonials.

"Please give a testimonial because you believe this seminar has helped you and will benefit others. I will give you a signed copy of my book in return. Please, don't do it for the gift but

because you believe (that's the emotional passion connection again) in the benefits of this seminar."

He received many testimonials with this request. Think about what you can offer your customers as a "thank you" for the plug.

▶ *How-To/Demonstrations:* This style is the most popular and most beneficial for building trust and loyalty. It can be offered for free on your YouTube channel or website. You can require a subscription (great for you to provide special benefits to your existing loyal customers). Make sure you know what you want the viewer to be able to do after watching the video. Do not try to cover more than ONE point per video. You will get more people to watch 5, 3-minute videos than to get one person to sit through one 15-minute video. Demonstrations differ from "how-to" in that you are demonstrating one complete product or service offering. If you are demonstrating a stain remover, show it being used on clothes, furniture, and rugs. Think <u>Billy Mays</u> commercial. If you are demonstrating how to groom and poof your dog, show the entire step-by-step process. Make sure you illustrate the process from beginning to end. Demonstrations are similar to a commercial. Commercials are less than 3 minutes. Cut out the boring parts during editing.

I include promotions as part of the demonstration style category. Promote a new book you've just

written. Find a nice chair and read a page or two from your great fiction novel. Think of being as comfortable as <u>Mrs. Doubtfire</u> at the end of the movie of the same name. If you are selling a business or non-fiction book, set the stage with an opening that asks one or two questions where the viewer will think "Yes, that's me." Similar to my "Get Published" introduction in the planning section of this book.

▶ *Informational:* For reviews, make sure you have a picture or are standing in front of what you are talking about. If you are reviewing a restaurant, have a picture of either the inside or outside of the restaurant. If you are talking about ways to save money while traveling through Italy, include pictures of attractions in Italy. Use this style of video to provide information or trivia. Make it entertaining. Make it visual.

▶ *Interviews:* Have at least **10 questions** in mind. You probably won't get to ask that many in a 3 minute video. It is better to be over-prepared than under-prepared. Ask questions you KNOW the interviewee can answer. If you are unsure, share your questions ahead of time. You want the interviewee to be comfortable. You want the interviewee to be pleased as well. If he or she is pleased with the finished video, the interviewee will forward the video to his or her customers...thus spreading the word about YOU!

Make sure when you are talking to the interviewee, you are looking at the interviewee. When the interviewee is answering you, have him or her look at the audience...which, in this case, means the little red light on the camera. In other words, talk to the audience. As the interviewee talks, you look at the interviewer, not the audience or your notes (unless you will zoom yourself out of the frame when editing). If you are interviewing someone, your eye contact should change. Your guest needs to look at the camera. You need to look at your guest. When you are talking to the audience, then you look at the camera. Look at whom you are listening or talking to at all times. The viewer should always be the most important character in the video. Your audience is the main character. In this video style, your interviewee is the second main character...you are the least important...you are the means, the glue between the guest and the audience.

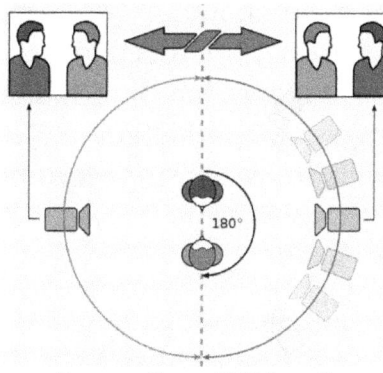

Image from Wikipedia
(180 degree rule)
(See hyperlink table in the back of the book)

If you are using more than one camera, make sure the cameras are pointing in the same direction and not at each other. This is the 180 degree rule of thumb. From Wikipedia.org: *"The* **_180° rule_** *is a basic guideline in film*

making that states that two characters (or other elements) in the same scene should always have the same left/right relationship to each other. If the camera passes over the imaginary axis connecting the two subjects, it is called **crossing the line***. The new shot, from the opposite side, is known as a* **reverse angle***."*

Image means an invisible line between you and the guest you are interviewing. That invisible line can NOT be crossed or be between the cameras. In other words, you have all the cameras facing in front of you, pointing at you from the same side of the line.

No need to download or transfer to your computer after every take. Watch the take on the camera. Look for major faux pas (like taping ½ of your interviewee off camera). Learn from that mistake and video again immediately afterwards. After three takes you will have enough to piece together for a great video. No one is expecting perfection. Your viewers are looking for information not cinema. Unplanned imperfection illustrates authenticity and builds trust with the viewers.

Presentation Checklist

You've created your video strategy. You've planned out your videos. You've even practiced a bit to improve your video presence. Let's go through the presentation checklist to make sure you are ready to process the videos you take.

- ☑ Do you have the right hardware/software to start?
- ☑ Do you have my points in front of you out of view?
- ☑ Are you ready for inside or outside environment? Nothing distracting in the way (sound)?
- ☑ How's the lighting?
- ☑ How's the video recorder(s) set up?
- ☑ Do you know where to stand (AND STAY PUT)?
- ☑ Is your stage area clean of unwanted images, sounds?
- ☑ Is your outfit clean and presentable?
- ☑ Is the audio clear?
- ☑ Do you know your opening and closing statements?

Scene 5: Process

You've planned your video strategy. You've done some takes. Now it is time to create your video masterpiece. If you know the message and point of the video, it is really easy with the software available today to create a valuable video. You have different options you can employ during the editing process to make a blah video just that much more viral (aka others spreading the word about you and your video).

Editing

The finished video you create may come from many different takes. It may require the insertion of explanatory slides with voice overrides. The editing software (one or many) will help you create a story from the series of video takes, photographs and text. Variety is the spice of video...too much, however, will dilute your message. All of these editing suggestions are optional. I've seen video's with some of these, all of these, and none of these editing suggestions. It is really up to you what you add to create the story you want your audience to hear and VALUE. Keep these basics in mind as you create your videos that demonstrate your value.

> ► ***Concise Your Message:*** There will be times when you create a video you will decide something you said isn't important but it is part of the same take where some important information appears. Have no fear...just trim it out. You can even cut out a long "ummmmmmmmmm" if you accidently

started thinking out loud during the take. The occasional filler words which are short, leave in. We're talking about the occasional "you know", "ah", "ok." If you cut all of them out of your video your video may look choppy. Instead, practice more for your *next* video.

▶ ***Title Slides:*** First off, title slides are not necessary. Jeffrey Gitomer rarely uses title slides. He instead uses his opening line (often times a question) to grab the audience attention. He has a grabber for a closing slide as well.

It's ok to have an opening and closing slide. Try to keep them to less than 10 seconds. If it is only one slide with no action, keep it under 5 seconds.

o The opening should contain the title of the video (and series). Don't worry about your name and contact information yet. You want your title to grab the attention of the audience. If it is a series, make the opening the same creating a consistent brand. Alan Weiss does the branding well with his "Writing on the Wall" series. You

Pat & Alan Weiss
(link address provided in Hyperlink Table at the end of the book)

only have 2-3 minutes to make a sale with the audience (i.e. to get them to trust you or promote you). <u>Patricia Fripp</u> uses the following scenario (paraphrased) when she trains CEOs to speak.

> *Think about what revenue your client will obtain from a new customer over a year may be. Divide that number by the length of your video. For example, a new customer would bring in $10,000 over a year. Your target video will be 3 minutes...which is 180 seconds. $10,000/180 = $55.56 per second. Is your 10 second introduction with your name and contact information worth $555.60 to your potential customer?*

o The closing slide can contain your contact information and have your call to action. If you provided valuable information already, the viewer will be happy to act on your call to action if he or she feels if value was received from watching your video. Include the call to action by leaving a comment, liking the video, and visiting your "landing page."

▶ ***Photographs:*** Images are better than a solid background. They are especially good for title slides, or still images of what you do (a cake, a

Picture from the
Get Published Video Series

store front, you winning a triathlon). Sizing of the image is also important. You want to make sure your slide doesn't look "stretched." Make sure your images are 320 x 220 pixels at a 180 dpi (dots per inch or pixals per inch) resolution for YouTube. With my photograph printing background (ScarletsFeathers.com), I tend to work in a higher resolution. I have succeeded in creating an image size of 4.5" x 3.38" @ 300 dpi for images with a fine level of detail. With the exception of the Library of Congress photograph and the typewriter eraser sculpture, I use images where the image is on one side of the slide and a blank or plain colored background fills the space.

In this example, I created an image slide to be inserted multiple times in a single video and in the video series. The picture enhanced the detail at the 300 dpi resolution. I added text via the video editor on the left every time I used this slide. This developed consistency and a visual reminder of The Get Published brand.

There are sites available where you can purchase an image. The same rules of usage apply as with the music discussed further in this section. Google "royalty free images" and a description of the type of image you are looking for (beach, sports field) to find an image you may be able to use. HINT: If you want people to remember YOU, and your product or service, take your own photographs and create title slides from your images.

▶ ***Zooming:*** If you have an unwanted view in your great take (a squirrel climbing a nearby tree), think about "cutting it out" without losing your great material. You can zoom in to remove any distracting background action. Also, close-ups and pan-outs add comfort for the viewer rather than a hard transition between one take and another. It also adds variety avoiding the static photography mindset. If you have a long section, think about zooming in or out to focus the attention on what is important. Zooming adds interest to your video. Zooming (as with changing the camera angle) helps refocus the viewers' attention from potential wandering. Remember to keep what may be necessary (i.e. pointing to a picture or hand movement) in view. Take 0.5 to 2 seconds to transition to the desired point. Be careful not to do it too often. You may make your audience "sea-sick".

▶ ***Adding your brand:*** If you have a logo, add it in the corner of your video in a .png image format.

Small and discreet is the goal. It is a "watermark" discreetly placed and will be absorbed by the viewer without taking away from your message. (Some video editing services include their logo; requiring a fee to remove their logo.) It is also okay to add your website or landing page towards the bottom of your video. It will be noticed more if it appears and disappears. It is not important to put 'http://www.' anymore. Especially since the "brand" is an image and not clickable. (NOTE: we'll talk about when you do need to provide the http://www. when discussing posting.)

Warning: YouTube annotations can appear anywhere. The most common placement is on the bottom. Keep this in mind when you are adding your logo. You do not want to cover over anything important with a YouTube annotation.

▶ ***Adding text:*** If your video is showing action, add text to appear at the time, the exact time, one of your features appears. For example, if your product has unique features, add text or an arrow to reinforce the point about them. As the customers use the product, the features occurred. Text can be added (and at one point even an arrow to point to the specific action) to illuminate the product feature. On the <u>Get Published series</u>, I placed an arrow pointing to the entry way of the US Library of Congress along with the inspiring text stating the viewer's book could be in the US Library of Congress.

How To Get Published: Episode 21 Additional resources video

sbdipat 43 videos Subscribe

This video is public.

Get Published Video Series
(link address provided in Hyperlink Table at the end of the book)

A thoughtfully placed bullet point summarizing the point you are making is an excellent visual note to the viewer to help them remember. This is especially good for "how to" videos. If you are cooking a sauce, remind the viewer the amount of butter or flour you are adding with text to appear just as you are adding the ingredient. Make sure the color and the size of the text is seen over the action in the video.

Think about adding a reminder in the middle of your video of your website. A short 2 second "Visit Viditude.com for more videos" adds a simple reminder in case someone does not watch the

entire video. This can also be added using YouTube clickable annotations (notice the blue strip at the bottom of the previous video). Make sure you do NOT leave important text or call-outs ¼" from the bottom. This would be covered over when you add YouTube annotations.

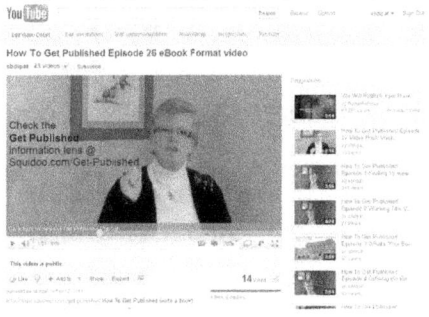

Get Published Video Series Episode 26
(link address provided in Hyperlink Table at the end of the book)

▶ **Transitions:** I'm not a big fan of jumping from one shot to the next. I prefer a smooth transition. Some software allows you to add in different types of transitions. Being a reader and published author, my personal favorite is the "page turn" sensation. Keep the transitions short, preferably less than a second (I use between .3 and 1 second). The purpose of transitions is to make the switch easy on the viewer's eyes and provide a mental note that you are changing gears.

► ***Music:*** There is plenty of royalty free music available. Royalty free does not mean free. You need to purchase the music (or use files that came with your video editing software). You can USE it based upon the "<u>creative commons</u>" license. Most of the music for a basic use (you aren't making any money off the use of the music) costs between $5 and $30. IF (this is a big IF) you are creating a video which will be SOLD (creating a DVD of a seminar or speech you presented), you will have to pay more for a license, maybe between $50 and $100 (more for custom music). Here is a link to a simple explanation of <u>usage terms for AudioJungle</u> (the site I use to purchase theme music).

o Select the right sound which reflects your brand. For example, a yoga studio may want soothing music but a cross-fit gym will prefer a hard-core rock tune.

o Select music you can hear over and over and over again. If your video provides valuable information, your customer will be watching it multiple times. If your viewer gets sick of the music, he or she will stop watching your video. Once you start creating a video series, you will be using the same music as a means to create an audio-signal to your brand. Make sure you can hear the music over and over and over again too.

o Adjust the volume to ensure the music does not override any of your talking. Keep the music at the 100% volume during any title slides and 15% during long transitions. Otherwise, keep the music down to about 3% to 10% as background music. Remember to fade the volume to prevent any jolts to the viewer senses. If the music you purchased as an opening, a middle and an ending, align properly to your video or if the music is longer than your video, cut out the audio from the music during the low volume area background during talking. If you need to repeat your section, repeat just the middle, using the low volume area to link the different music sections.

▶ ***Rendering:*** The final step in editing is rendering. This is the process of creating your video for posting. The software will ask which destination you are creating your video to be viewed. I usually select PC which will work for YouTube but may not be good for HD TV. It depends on where your target audiences will most likely view your video. If you are creating custom dimensions, rendering at YouTube recommended 720 x 480 is fine (this avoids your video being "stretched" during export. The result on YouTube will be about 75%. In the beginning, let the software you use define the rendering.

Once your video rendering is done, then it's time to preview it on your computer. Preview it on your

computer before uploading to make sure it is clean, and all your effects are exactly as expected.

Editing Step-By-Step Summary

Now that you understand all the options available to take your video to the next level, let me summarize. Below are the 10 steps in the order I follow to edit all my videos.

1. Brighten/Darken any videos I plan on using in one software.
2. Save the file in a lower resolution if necessary.
3. Import all video takes I'll be combining into one video.
4. Import the separate audio file if I have one and align it to the visual.
5. Edit each video to make one story.
6. Add zoom to move a person to the tic-tac-toe point of view (or eliminate any unnecessary background).
7. Add text (call outs) to emphasize a point.
8. Add title slides.
9. Add transition slides.
10. Add music.
11. Save the file with a filename using keywords that describe my video. Not doing so was a BIG mistake I made with my first video series "Get Published". Once your file is uploaded, you cannot change the raw file name. I uploaded raw files with a file name that made sense to me and not the general public. (WAPEpisode20.mp4). If I had

changed it to Get Published Episode 1, I would have increased the search ability.

Remember to render for the environment in which the video will most likely be viewed. If possible, test your video on different PCs, smartphones and tablets to see how it will be viewed by others.

We will talk about annotations during posting. This is a YouTube only (and FABULOUS) feature.

Process Checklist

You've taken multiple takes for your video. You are about to process (edit) your video to create a compelling story your viewers will want to watch to the end.

- ☑ Do you have enough sufficient takes to create a video story?
- ☑ Did you purchase or create images you can use inside the video to reinforce my brand?
- ☑ Do you have the right music which matches the mood and tone of the video?
- ☑ Do you have the proper level of rights?
- ☑ Where would zooming add emphasis to what I'm saying?
- ☑ Are the timings of transitions good?
- ☑ Are the transitions smooth?
- ☑ Did you cut out anything which is essential to convey my message and story?
- ☑ What text can you include to add another sense of understanding of what you are saying or demonstrating?
- ☑ Does the video flow?
- ☑ Did you render to the typically viewed environment.

Scene 6: Post

The big gorilla for online video is <u>YouTube</u>. No matter where you post your video, YouTube has to be number one. Once you post it there, you can link to it throughout your social media presence. If you wish to have your video on multiple video sites, <u>Tubler</u> or <u>TubeMogul</u> can be used to reach other video sites like <u>Blip.TV</u>, <u>Vimeo</u>, <u>Viddler</u>, and many others. In the beginning...stick with YouTube. After you are comfortable with YouTube, then follow <u>Steve Garfield's book *Get Seen* advice</u>. He provides the most concise and complete explanation of all your options and how to use them (including getting your videos on CNN).

Think twice about loading your video on your own website. The bandwidth needed and the support of your videos is huge. Use <u>YouTube</u> or <u>Amazon S3</u>. Think of your video in a 'cloud" managed and supported by a company which already has the bandwidth. Have the peace of mind to know you have a place that is managed for you and your videos will be available for your viewers.

The most popular days to upload videos are Friday, Saturday, and Sunday. Don't allow your video to get lost in the crowd, upload a different day of the week...preferably in the morning.

Loading Your Video on YouTube

Here is the simple step-by-step process I use for each video on YouTube. If I only have one video, I still add it

to a playlist because I only show "playlists" on my channel. Therefore, even individual videos will have its own playlist. NOTE: Turn off your connections with other social networks if you are uploading more than one video. Your followers only need to be reminded once...not every 5 minutes.

Step By Step YouTube Edit Process

Here is my process you can follow with every video you upload to YouTube.

1. Sign into your YouTube channel.
2. Select Upload Video.
3. Click on the video you wish to upload.
4. Add a title (with a keyword most searched for that applies to your video in the title). For a series, provide the following information within 60 characters title: The series name: Episode # video title and finally the word "video". For example: How to Write a Book: Episode 5 Chapter Premise Video (total 52 characters).
   a. The series name was "How To Write A Book:".
   b. Followed by the word Episode and the number (5).
   c. Followed by the Episode title, Chapter Premise.
   d. Ending with Video (because "video" is a popular search term).
5. In the description area (up to 5,000 characters is permitted by YouTube):

a. Begin with your web address in URL format (http://www.yourwebsite.com). Without the http://www. your website will NOT be clickable.

b. Repeat your title.

c. Describe what the viewer will learn in your video using as many search terms that apply in the first 22 words (what is seen by the viewer without selecting "more").

d. Add as much information about the video you can in the remaining characters. You include common search terms that are applicable to the video. You can include closely related terms (i.e. publish a book) that someone may use to search for a similar video series.

e. For longer videos (more than 5 minutes), add video times (i.e. 00:20). The times will automatically become a jump-to-link (hyperlink) to specific points in the video (like a table of contents).

f. Repeat your title.

6. In the Tag section, add common search terms which apply to your video topic.

a. Include your name in quotes ("Pat Ferdinandi", "Patricia Ferdinandi").

b. Include your primary business function (speaker).

c. If you do not know what "tags" are used, you can search for related videos and see what search terms they use and select what YouTube recommends, if they apply.

d. You can also use Google to identify tags. Begin a "Google search" and see what shows in the drop down list in Google recommended searches list.

e. Pick related keywords or tags. If you are demonstrating particular pasta sauce (Fra Diablo sauce), add other common sauce (Vodka sauce) names in your tag section.

f. If a tag or suggested keyword doesn't pertain to you...do not add it. Google will flag you as spam.

7. Select the most appropriate category for your video. For example, select "how to" for demonstration; select "educational" for testimonials. Not the best fit, but it works. Education and entertainment videos are the most popular on YouTube. Use these categories ONLY IF IT FITS. Attempting to fake the social engine will backfire.

8. Add the date of your video was created or uploaded.

9. Add your location under YouTube location...especially important for local business searches.

10. At this moment, you make your video "private" (second option under broadcasting and sharing options) requiring a link to see your video until you go through the next YouTube set up process.

11. Save your YouTube video.

Once your video has been loaded and registered into YouTube (anywhere between 5 minutes and a day), it is time to go back and edit your video for a second time.

1. Double check that all the information you previously entered, stuck.

2. Select the one of 3 thumbnail images which best describes your video. Unfortunately, you cannot create your own thumbnail image and give it to YouTube. All you get to select is one of the three options they provide. If possible, keep the theme (similar thumbnails) for a series or pick a thumbnail which displays an important point viewers will want to learn.

3. Save your YouTube video.

Annotations

Annotation is extremely important. Annotation is a YouTube function which allows you to add a clickable link to your video. Currently, the clickable link must be to some place within YouTube. However, the options are fabulous for "call of action" which keeps your viewer involved. The most important type of annotations is adding a YouTube annotation "NOTE."

If your video is part of a series, add a note which links to the previous video at the beginning of the timeline. This provides the viewer an option to go back and see previous videos in the series. Towards the end of the

video timeline, add a "note" to automatically start the next video in the series. For both of these options, make sure you check off the "link" box and add the YouTube "video" link type and provide the actual YouTube shareable video link address.

If this video is part of a series, add a "note" towards the end of the video to link to the entire playlist. Make sure you check off the "link" box and add the YouTube "playlist" link type and provide the actual YouTube shareable playlist link address.

Someplace in the middle of the video, add a "subscribe" option. Make sure you check off the "link" box and select the "subscribe" link type and provide your YouTube channel address.

Notes are commonly seen on the bottom of the video across the entire video screen. You will have to move the text box down for all of the above notes. Choose a color combination which matches your brand and is easily readable. Otherwise, stick to the YouTube default black/white. Take a look at my Get Published series of video. For all of the notes, I selected a blue color band with yellow text. This color combination was the closest match to the company Strategic Business Decisions and Viditude color scheme and video.

Select the "save" button after every annotation is added. This is just a safety precaution in case you get called away or you have any PC/Mac problems.

Once all of the annotations have been added, you can select the "publish" button.

After you have annotated all the videos you uploaded and edited in YouTube, remember to:

1. Make your video "public". This is the first option under "broadcasting and sharing". This is important for making your video searchable and provides additional "Google Juice".

2. Allow comments and voting. Your goal is to build a community of followers. About 1% of your best followers will comment. More will vote up/down. The more comments and votes, the more "Juice" you will have in Google search.

3. Allow embedding. You will want to embed your video to your website, blog, Facebook and other social media sites. Your business partners may also wish to embed your video. Your fans may wish to talk about you and add a link. Be accessible and you will increase your "juice" and following.

4. Re-link your connections to all your other social media sites (Facebook & Twitter especially). YouTube will notify your following on each network you have saved/uploaded/liked a new video. You can "like" your own video ONCE to initiate YouTube to post a status. Don't "like" or notify of posting more than one video a day. Your following gets annoyed receiving multiple notifications in less than a day.

To learn more about annotations and how to use them, watch a <u>YouTube educational video</u>. Make sure you add annotations to all your videos. YouTube is owned by Google. This adds "Google Juice" to your videos.

Playlist and Channel Optimization

Keep in mind that search engine optimization applies to your playlist and channel descriptions and tags as they do with your video. Make sure you pick meaningful tags and descriptions for every playlist as well as your YouTube channel. Include your name, product name, and company name within "quotes" as potential Google search terms.

Insight Power

Who is watching your videos? Insight provides great demographic information about who watches your channel, playlists, and individual videos. If you are not reaching the demographic you identified as your potential customer, you may need to tweak your message. Once a month, take a look at the statistics Google captures and provides to you about your YouTube videos, playlists, and channel. YouTube Insights lets you see how long it takes for your video to become popular (and viral), and how that video performs once it reaches a certain popularity status. Here's a <u>YouTube Insight tutorial</u> describing the basic insight features.

Branding Your Page

Think about having a common "look" on all your social media destinations to reinforce your brand. This is accomplished by branding (creating a common background theme and font colors) page for each of the social destinations (YouTube Channel, Blog Page, and Twitter). This is going to be a trial and error. You will need to create a different image with different dimensions for each social media site (Twitter, YouTube, Blog). Get friends who own a different type of PC and width to send you a "screen print" to make sure your image looks good on different width PCs. Check your branded page on your PC/Mac, a notebook/macbook, and tablet and smartphone (Droid/iPhone) if possible. Or, visit a computer store and go to your site. Warning: When I created backgrounds and tested it...I forgot I had my zoom at least 125%. Test all background images for 100% and 125% (for us older folks).

Once you have branded your pages, make sure you list your blog and channel with important search engines such as:

- ► Google: http://www.google.com/addurl/
- ► Yahoo: http://search.yahoo.com/info/submit.html
- ► Bing:
  http://www.bing.com/webmaster/submitsitepage.a
  spx
- ► Not for profit:
  http://www.dmoz.org/help/submit.html

YouTube Channel Branding

Twitter and YouTube allow you to add a custom background. The two other big dogs of social networking, <u>Facebook</u> and <u>LinkedIn</u>, don't offer background customization options. Facebook does allow you to have a custom "home tab" in which you can embed a "welcome" video. To learn more, follow the Facebook expert, <u>Mari Smith.</u>

The key difference between YouTube and Twitter background is where to focus your logo, brand, and image. Whereas your Twitter background should be focused as far to the left as possible, the content in your YouTube background should be as close to the central band of content as possible without going behind it. Facebook does allow you to change your landing page. This requires knowledge of Facebook's special HTML code. Businesses do use this feature for a "welcome" or "call to action" video. Think about it...then hire a specialist.

Twitter requires a background image to be less than 800k. Your image must be in a .gif, .jpg, or .png format. I recommend a .png format and save your image with the *interlaced* option selected. You can upload your custom image under the Twitter->Settings->Design section. After you upload your customized image, check the "tile" box to have your image repeat. You will need to play with the image size and upload several times to find the right size for your image not to be covered by the new Twitter home page. Especially if you are attempting to have a specific image appear on each side of the Twitter feed.

The size of the Viditude Twitter background image is 626 x 420 pixels @ 72dpi. Once you are happy with the look of your customized background, feel free to customize the colors for text, sidebars, and links to reinforce your brand colors.

Your YouTube channel background can go up to 2000 pixels width by up to 2200 pixels in length @ 72 dpi (dots per inch). Make sure you keep the middle (7.5" to 20") blank for the YouTube videos. Keep ALL images close to the 7.5" and 20" line to support the different screen sizes. Take a look at <u>Viditude's YouTube Channel</u> background. I mention I can be found on other major social networks. You will notice the images are repeating down the sides only. This is accomplished by making the length shorter. The image is 633 pixels. If you do repeat, do not use a gradient background or you will incorporate a line. Instead, pick a single background which will also blend into your YouTube theme colors. Also keep in mind the size of your monitor versus that of your viewers. Because widescreen monitors may view much more of your image on the left and right, it may be useful to incorporate a fade to a solid color on each end. Then make the page background that same color to avoid an unsightly "break" in the design. Leave the images close to the center but not covered by the YouTube display area.

Where Are You Socially

YouTube is only a small part of the social media landscape. The viral-ability of your YouTube video is dependent upon you initiating the spreading across your

social networks. It is important to help spread the word about your video by building your "link juice". This requires you to provide links to your YouTube channel, playlist, and individual videos all across your social media presence. Luckily, YouTube makes linking very easy.

Your social engagement journey will grow over time with the effort you put into your digital "social" footprint. AntsEyeView.com, a marketing strategy company, provides a great evaluation to determine your level of commitment (and eventual success) to your social media campaign.

Embedding Your YouTube Video

Linking to a specific video is better than reposting your video. Google Juice for a video increases as the number of links to a video increases. If you repost your video, you are reducing the potential amount of "Google Juice". If you link from various places (Twitter, Facebook, blog) you will increase your Google Juice while reaching the same audience if you had reposted your video on the various social media sites.

A simple way to get a link to your video is to create a blog write up or post around your video content and then link to the video in your post. Make sure you add a transcript of your video in the blog post. Google is a TEXT search engine. Software does exist to translate your audio into text. It's not the greatest. It will require significant corrections. Otherwise, you can hire a

transcriber to do this for you. See our resource listing at the end of this book.

An RSS (Really Simple Syndication) feed is a family of <u>web feed</u> formats used to publish frequently updated works. A customer can request an RSS feed to your blog to make sure he or she keeps up to date. An RSS feed is different from an email. An RSS feed allows your customer to organize what he or she wants to stay on top. Every time you post something new to your blog, a "headline" will appear on a Google or Yahoo tab along with all the other RSS feeds your customer has requested. The RSS feed saves your customer time by having all the latest and greatest information available in one place versus having to go to several websites just to inquire if anything new has been posted.

IF (a big IF) you have content your customer considers worth following, you will need to enable the ability for your customer to request an RSS feed of your blog. More advanced technology-skilled people may wish to create an RSS feed option. More information about <u>"How to Create a YouTube RSS Feed/API"</u> is available from YouTube. Here is a link to the specific YouTube tutorial video.

Your Facebook Connection

Should you load your video separately to Facebook? Or, should you provide a "link" to your video in a newsfeed? Frankly, both. The "link" provides more Google Juice for the specific video. The Facebook newsfeed status, however, is temporary and can easily get lost.

If your video is short (less than 15 minutes), it is good to load your video into Facebook for more permanence. The comments people provide (along with the "likes") stay with the video you uploaded to Facebook.

Your Facebook connection to your blog is important. Facebook provides a "like" button which adds to your "Google Juice". Thanks to 1GoodReason (Chris Kieff), I discovered Facebook had 2 separate "like" buttons which performed differently. One Facebook "Like" button makes you a fan of a page, the other merely puts a mention of a website onto your wall to be put into your friends' newsfeed. One is a permanent connection between you and a business in Facebook, the other is a one time, "hey look at this" passing mention. And they are both called "Like", look identical and are virtually indistinguishable. Chris provides a great explanation on this post on 1GoodReason. Bottom line, you will want to use both buttons (with the Facebook image) throughout any blog post.

You can provide "tags" to people in your "friends" network. This provides a newsfeed in their profile. Don't overdo this feature. People are very protective of what they want on their newsfeed...even if they are in the video.

You may have a direct link from YouTube to your Facebook account. This provides the newsfeed that you uploaded, liked, commented on the video. If you are loading a separate version directly into Facebook, do it

about 3 days after you loaded it on YouTube. People use social media on different days at different times.

Posting Checklist

Now that you loaded your first video, it's time to check that everything is in place to promote your premier.

- ☑ Do you have a social presence on YouTube, Facebook, LinkedIn, Twitter?
- ☑ Is your branding done on YouTube and Twitter?
- ☑ Is your video on YouTube?
- ☑ Does your video have all the description information added?
- ☑ Are all the annotations in place?
- ☑ Did you select the best thumbnail?
- ☑ Is your video public?
- ☑ Did you load a separate video on Facebook and Flickr?
- ☑ What other video sites can you upload your video?

Scene 7: Promote

Waiting to be found didn't even work for <u>Snowball</u> the dancing cockatoo. Snowball became famous because Irena shared the video link with a few friends via email. The parrot community is very well connected. The parrot-loving community sent the link via many different forums. Facebook was growing in popularity. The link was shared there before <u>Bird Lovers Only</u> had their Facebook page set up. Eventually, an article was written about Snowball in the most popular bird magazine, <u>Bird Talk</u>. That is where I first heard about Snowball. I proceeded, like so many others, to share the link with both parrot-loving friends and those in my other communities.

Once your video has had a few hundred views, your video should start appearing on Google for your key phrase (tags). I was amazed at how quickly this occurred with the <u>Get Published video series</u>. It took less than a month even with heavy competition with the tag, "Get Published". This is because I took responsibility for spreading the word to my colleagues, customers, friends, relatives, and following.

Promotion is *your* responsibility.

How to Make Your Video Go Viral

Everyone wants to know the secret formula to get a video to go viral. Unfortunately, if everyone had a viral video, nothing would be different enough to be noticed. There is always an added element that is impossible to

predict...that of audience reaction. If you did your homework and know your primary target audience (where they are and what they want) you have an opportunity. The best you can do in an attempt to make a viral video is as follows:

1. Identify a topic known to be popular and associated with you, your product or service.
2. Determine what customers (including the extended fringe) need to know and want to hear about.
3. Develop a sincere, humorous (if appropriate) and inspirational way to convey the SINGLE message.
4. Film it in a unique or trendy style (wide angle, fisheye, slow motion).
5. Post it on YouTube.
6. Link it to all social media outlets.
7. Promote/share the heck out of it.

Start the Ball Rolling For Spreading the Good Word about You

"Build it and they will come." may have worked for Field of Dreams...it isn't enough for you. You need to start the ball rolling by notifying people the video exists. This is first done by alerting your community who will pass the word to their external community who will then pass the word to their other communities. The beauty of spreading the word now is the ease with which it can be accomplished to the many different social media outlets available FOR FREE.

Remember, social media is about the conversation within your community. If all you do is sell, you are NOT using social media correctly. The mistake so many people make is to use social media to talk AT people or use social media to distribution information outward. Successful social media is about creating a community and having a social conversation (with video). Here is post that contains a great list of what NOT to do by Don Snyder (Don The Idea Guy).

Pat & Gary Vaynerchuk

Watch Gary's
The Thank You Economy Book Signing Talk

(link address provided in Hyperlink Table at the end of the book)

Gary Vaynerchuk (author of Crush It and The Thank You Economy) discusses how Social Media can be used to personally thank all your friends, fans, subscribers, and connections. Gary Vaynerchuk (@GaryVee) illustrates how a small and large company can use social media (including YouTube) to build a community and have a personal conversation with thousands. I only discussed video in this book. The successful company will be the one who masters all the

components of social media to have a conversation with their community.

The best way to carry you and your business through the

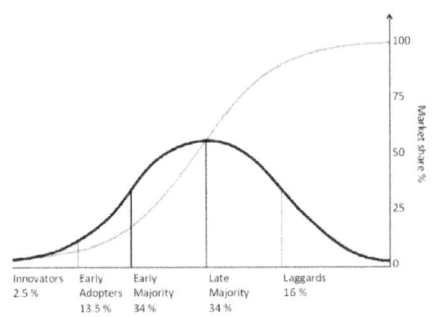

Image from Wikipedia
(Diffusion of innovations)

marketing curve is to find those to help you spread the word. Videos are a means to use your "early adopters" to spread the word about you. Through whatever means (digitally or other means) you need to create momentum by finding ten (10) fanatics or early adopters and supporters of you to help spread the word about you. Once you cross over 100, you will notice a difference in the search engine results and in being "found".

Your video will have a life. How long a life and how successful will depend first and foremost on the quality of the content (the story's emotional appeal and helpfulness). Secondly is how well you promote your video initially. Ron Ploff describes the three life phases as Blastoff, Booster, and Free Trajectory. Using Ron's terms, let me explain what you will see:

► *Blastoff:* Consider this the birth announcement. The excitement of the new video. How will you announce your video will initiate the viralness.
► *Booster:* Consider this the teenage years. Frustration as the interest wanes. It's not new but

still talked about IF your video is interesting and still adds *perceived* value.

▶ *Free Trajectory:* The middle-age of video. The interest in the video is steady and consistent unless some outside force propels interest. This is the long-tail of marketing. Only those serious in what you offer will continue to find and watch you. THESE ARE YOUR MOST LOYAL (POTENTIAL) CUSTOMERS. Continue to cater to them!

Your Digital Footprint

It is important to start building links back to your video. The more websites which link back to your video on YouTube, the more relevant that video will appear in searches. You have a wide variety of sources to link to your video. You have email, Facebook, LinkedIn, Squidoo, Twitter, and Blog available to help you spread the word about your video. These link sources are the "must use" after YouTube. You probably have at least one of these facilities (email). Try to get as many as possible. It's important that you set up your digital footprint as you start creating videos and before you send out messages about them. If you mention your YouTube channel with the link, search engine optimization (SEO) requires http://www.youtube.com/**USER**/channelname.

▶ *Email:* The electronic means of communicating directly to one or more customers. If properly monetized, one email will generate $1.00US per month. A "value message" (with a video link) should be sent out at least once a month. Have a

signature on all emails which contain your name, telephone number, address, and website (where your videos will be for your followers to see). Send out a value message via an electronic email newsletter (eZine) to your following using a tool like <u>Constant Contact</u> or <u>AceOfSales</u>. Include a video picture with the text translation. Your goal is to have your following go to your website. Put only a paragraph or two of the article with a "read more" link to your website. Add a link to the video from the picture which also takes you to your website. A GREAT example of the use of eZines is <u>Jeffrey Gitomer's Sales Caffeine</u>. Sign up for it...it's free.

► *Facebook:* Let's face it...Facebook will be around for a long time. Here is a list of the 10 Reasons to use Facebook for marketing summarized from <u>RealSEO.com</u>:

1. ***Audience:*** Facebook is the 2nd largest trafficked website, with over 500 million active users.
2. ***Referrals:*** Facebook is the 2nd largest referral source for video.
3. ***Mobile:*** 150 million active users take Facebook with them everywhere they go.
4. ***Time:*** Many people spend a lot more time on Facebook than on Google
5. ***Versatility:*** Many video formats are supported for uploading

6. **Length:** Facebook allows up to 20 minutes, 5 minutes more than YouTube

7. **Connectivity***:* It has a wide range of sharing features and engagement opportunities. While Facebook doesn't let you share its content on other social networks (like YouTube and Twitter), because of its large member base, you will certainly have many more connections from the onset that may lead to better sharing potential.

8. **Search Engine Visibility:** Facebook videos are visible within Google Search.

9. **SMO** (Social Media Optimization): Excellent keyword encoding (aka, "tagging") capabilities.

10. **Conversions***:* Hot triggers around the video for taking an intended action.

You must have a personal Facebook page associated with a single email account. Once established, you can create a "business" Facebook page. It is on this Facebook page where you will be posting about your latest products, services, videos, testimonials. Post something of interest and of value to your customers at least once a week. You can load your YouTube video separately or provide a status update with a YouTube link on a regular basis. You may wish to do both.

Create a Welcome Landing Page with a welcome video message (and a couple of testimonials). Tell your customers what they will have access to on your website/squeeze page (free downloads,

coupons, information) when they leave Facebook to go to your site. Remember your "call to action". Ask the Facebook visitor to "Like" your page. Here is a video on YouTube explaining how to customize your <u>Facebook landing page.</u>

► *LinkedIn:* Every individual consultant or professional has a page listing his or her strengths, career path, and what they do. You can add a "Slideshare" application which basically allows you to upload a PowerPoint-type presentation. LinkedIn currently does NOT support video links. You can embed them through the Slideshare application in one of four ways:

1. By directly embedding your video into a PowerPoint presentation.

2. Creating just the title slide, upload the presentation to Slideshare, then add your "YouTube" link to your video after the title slide.

3. Or, you can add a news item on the appropriate discussion group with a link to your YouTube video.

4. Regular status updates point to your post/video.

► *Squidoo:* This is the best well-kept secret around. You can build a static website in less than half an hour. You can add a YouTube widget for your latest

video. What's important is <u>Squdioo</u> comes on the first page of search results. A YouTube widget allows you to "select yourself" up to ten videos per widget. You provide the exact "share this video" link from YouTube. If your series has more than 10 videos, have no fear. You can add as many YouTube widgets as you wish. Check out the <u>Get Published</u> Squidoo lens as an example.

▶ *Twitter:* The 140 character broadcast system to allow all those who follow to know you have a new video. You can plan ahead by using a tool like <u>SocialOomph</u> or <u>HootSuite</u>. The free versions allow you to set up tweets in advance. Identify when your target audience reads tweets (more in the morning, afternoon, or evening by time zone). Set up multiple tweets to point to specific video's on a regular basis to tweet at the time your followers will see them. Twitter now allows videos to play on your Twitter home page. Just click the video link and the video will play on the right "preview" pane. The standard life of a tweet is only 5 minutes.

▶ *Website/Blog:* This is your primary landing page for all about you. Facebook, Squidoo, YouTube are mirrors of your Website/Blog. It is this landing page where you keep the history of all your videos and important value messages. After all, you want to have your customers email address, not YouTube. Search engines like Google search on text. Pictures (like the one of your video) do go to the top of the page but your video will be found via

text. It is important to have text with your video. This is best accomplished on a blog. Put your video with as close as an exact transcription as possible (see resources at the end of this book) of your talk in a post. You can leave out any filler words.

Have all other social media mentions come back to your page. Make sure you include something on the sidebar to have something for your followers or finders to BUY. Keep it simple. As <u>Jeffrey Gitomer</u> always says: *Customers don't like to be sold but love to buy.* Your goal is to build a trusting relationship with every potential and existing customer. Overselling destroys that trust. Remember also NOT to automatically start your video. A customer may be at work or surfing late at night and still have the sound turned on their PC. People get annoyed if a video automatically starts on a website, blog or anything other than YouTube.

► *Video Sitemap:* Search engines are the biggest referrer to video content. Making your video "universal search friendly" is key to your video being discovered. Google, of course, is the primary search engine and the owner of YouTube). Google has a product which creates an expanded <u>mRSS</u> (Media Really Simple Syndication) feed called a <u>Video Sitemap</u>. It is the single best way to make Google aware of all your videos. The <u>Video Sitemap</u> provides information about your video to Google. Some of the information (<u>format description found here</u>) for every video includes:

- Video Title
- Video Description (all 5,000 characters)
- Play Page (where the video is located)
- Thumbnail Image Location (URL)
- Raw Video File Content Location
- Player Location (i.e.: if Adobe Flash is needed to play your video)
- Video Duration
- Video Expiration

A webmaster will create the special code for you after you provide the above information. If you are using WordPress, install a *Google Video Sitemap WordPress Plugin* to do the work for you.

Using Your Social Network (Email)

Now you have posted your video (first or for any future videos), it is important to let people know you've created something of value for them. Keep in mind that your friends, family, and colleagues want you to succeed (well, at least some of them). Your customers, clients, employers want to see you stay in business or employed. Ask for their help.

Send them a link to your video via email. Tell them this is a new video and you wish their opinion before you make it public. Tell them your video is going "live" in one week so they don't procrastinate with their comments. People, especially your loyal fans, want to be helpful. They just need a little reminder to do so.

Chances are a few of your email contacts are well connected and will spread the word for you. If your content is useful, they will look like providers and increase their personal value by passing on the link. This will only happen if your content is useful!

Don't abuse your connections. Everyone is stressed by the amount of information they need to read, listen, watch and absorb within their allotted time. You cannot send them a daily video. You cannot even send them a weekly video. Do share your first and maybe second videos over a month's time. After that, let them know you appreciate their assistance and have them sign up or subscribe to be notified of new content. Send them a HANDWRITTEN thank you. Yes, handwritten. It's rare, noticed, remembered, and talked about!

Using Your Customer's Network

Everyone needs help in getting noticed. Help your customers spread the word about them. Help them out by commenting on their Facebook business page, YouTube Video, Retweet their Tweet (or use the #FF for #followfriday recommendations), LinkedIn recommendation or talk about them in one of your videos. If they wrote a book, put a comment on Amazon (in text or video format). At minimum, become friends with your customers on wherever they are socially (Facebook, YouTube, LinkedIn, Twitter).

This is more than just "liking" their page. This is supplying something specific about them. Don't be

generic either. That comes across as insincere. Positive reinforcement always carries more weight than saying anything sarcastic or negative. Think about what you would want someone to say about you. You want to feel humbled afterwards. Pinpoint two specific points you really like about them or their product/service. It's about them...not you...so be sincere. You'll feel good for doing it, and you may actually get something reciprocated.

Don't forget about YouTube. YouTube typically displays thumbnails of the first four response videos. You can post a response to one of your client's videos. How good your response will allow your video's thumbnail to be associated with your customers' video longer and develop a life of its own. You will be able to ride the wave of their virability...IF IT IS GOOD AND HELPFUL.

The famous <u>United Breaks Guitars</u> by <u>Dave Carroll</u> went viral because of the viewer's emotions which were evoked. The <u>response by Taylor Guitars</u> latched onto United Breaks Guitars success. For some time, anyone viewing United Breaks Guitars saw Taylor's Response as one of the four thumbnail videos associated by YouTube. United Breaks Guitars raised the brand awareness of Taylor Guitar. Taylor Guitar leveraged the exposure with a **HELPFUL** response video.

Are any of your customers providing a video about you? The tone of the video doesn't matter. It's an opportunity for you. Are you taking advantage of it?

Using Other's Network

Having been an author of blogs (four at one time), I know how Fresh content is difficult to produce on a continual basis. Many bloggers are looking for guest posts or products to promote. These are great opportunities to help you grow your audience and expand your reach beyond your current community. If your post attracts visitors, receives "likes", is shared often, the blogger will be greatly appreciated. You provided them an expanded audience, a fresh voice, and a break for them. This is a win-win situation on both sides.

Find blogs that relate to your topic. Notice whether they ever use guest posts. Read their blog for a month to see the type of stories they are currently writing. Get an idea of the length of their typical posts (usually less than 250 words). Get to know which posts get the most comments. Get a picture of the demographics of their readership (some blogs explain their demographics "small business owners in the Chicago area" in their "about" page). Add comments (as you did with your customers) about a post you found valuable (and be sincere and specific). Finally, pitch your story to the editor in how it will be valuable to their readership. Then... make sure your content is GREAT and help spread the word when they post your piece.

There are a few public relations websites where you can submit a press release. PR Web is one of many. Another is eZine (for authors). Know your customer to narrow the distribution to the right audience. You do not want to do this for every video. Only do this when you have a new

product, service, or new video series. Press releases cost a varying amount of money.

Another good PR source that is unrelated to video is the Help A Reporter website. Submit your name as a source. You will receive 3 emails Monday through Friday. These are requests from small independent to large new organizations requesting information and examples. Respond with helpful information (never a sales pitch) and your name and company and website (your YouTube channel if you prefer) may be selected and used in its post, article, newspaper, magazine, book, or TV. If you are selected, a reader may want to find you, your blog, and your video. You never know. Oh, if you see something good for one of your customers to answer, send them an email. The secret to success is to become a trusted advisor. Once you achieved that level of appreciation, you develop loyal customers for life!

One last word on advertising on the Internet... you have Google Adwords and Facebook Ads. Do not do either unless you know your tags are right for your demographics. If you use either, try it for a very short period of time (set a dollar limit). You will be able to identify demographic information about your potential customers such as age, gender, likes, and job titles. This will be valuable in developing future ads, tags, or content for your videos.

Once Is Not Enough

The attention span on the Internet is quick. Tweets pass by quickly (typical life is 5 minutes). Facebook status updates and notifications pass quickly. In other words, your post may get lost as the tide moves in and out in the sea of Internet information. Your audience may never know about your video because the post came and went before they saw it. Therefore...posting once is not enough.

You need to repeat tweets and links to posts and videos (at different times of the day and week) to capture audience. Even the best video-bloggers Retweet (RT) their links to their posts. SocialOomph and HootSuite have a free version where you can set a time when a tweet is issued. Create a tweet for content a couple of times during the day of the first release and once a quarter *while the content is still relevant and valuable* to your community. Be careful about seasons. Don't post a link to a Christmas video in March.

Keeping Up With It All

Along the way in *Your Video Playbook*, we've mentioned some time-saving tips. There comes a time when you need to realize you may not have the time to do it all. You can hire help for every phase of the 7 P's Playbook. It's okay to try to do it all in the beginning to learn. It will help you select the right people to help you later.

Where is your time better spent? Everyone has the same 24 hours. You need to know how to spend your time

wisely to bring attention to you. Of course, <u>Viditude</u> is here to help you. I list other resources in the back of this book.

Let's face it. Social media is extremely time-consuming. New products come out daily. New venues which promote you take time to discover and use. The social media activities of promoting yourself and your videos will be your biggest consumer of your time. You save yourself social media time you can hire:

- ▶ An Internet Marketing company to help you manage your social media presence.
- ▶ A content manager or brand manager as a consultant or full-time employee.
- ▶ Someone, like <u>1GoodReason</u> to help you plan your entire social media strategy.
- ▶ Someone like <u>Becky Blanton</u> who will ghostwrite your articles and posts.
- ▶ Someone who can tweak or copywrite your material like <u>Jodi Kaplan</u>.
- ▶ Someone who will use the social media applications to promote the word about you.
- ▶ A company like <u>Pixability</u> or who will mail you a camera and edit what you've produced.
- ▶ A company like <u>Viditude</u> to help you plan, prepare, present, practice, prepare, post, and promote (the 7P's) YOU through video.

Just find people you will enjoy working with on a continual basis. Find people who believe in helping you achieve more customers, sales, and repeat business!

Whatever you decide to do, make sure the person or company has a social presence. Make sure they have a YouTube channel, a website/blog, a Facebook page, LinkedIn profile and all the other social sites where you want exposure. Make sure they understand the latest trend in search engine optimization. Understand the level of commitment. Will they be representing you in the Twitter or Facebook conversation? Do they provide examples of THEMSELVES in video (either through the company or personal channel)?

Keeping the Conversation Going

On all the social media avenues, you need to keep the conversation going. This goes beyond the posting, tweeting, status updates. This means responding to those who leave a comment, a like, or retweet (RT) your tweet. Every comment is a potential lead you can leverage. They already are following you, strengthen the conversation and relationship. You MUST follow-up to keep the conversation going by responding effectively and immediately to appropriate comments.

- ► *First* and foremost, you must be humble and thank them...let them know you appreciate them. AND...return the favor.

- ► *Secondly*, take the opportunity to offer them more related information. Send them a link to related videos. Let them know of any freebies you may have. This builds the brand of being a trusted advisor.

► ***Thirdly***, you can mention something available to buy. To quote <u>Jeff Gitomer</u>: *People don't like to be sold but they love to buy*. To add to <u>Jeffrey Gitomer's</u> quote, they will buy from you if they *trust* you. Do not make a commercial. Just mention you have something related for purchase. People may not know or remember some of your available products or services. Don't get discouraged quickly. It takes about 6-10 contacts (individual "touch" points) of trust before someone may purchase. They are not rejecting you, your offer just doesn't fit in their budget, time, or need right now.

Conversations do not always need to be on your digital turf. Find the appropriate LinkedIn discussion group to add comments of assistance (do not sell). Chat and engage with your customers on their Facebook page. The days of the neighborhood store has come back. It is just now in digital form.

How Is the Video Doing

There are certain metrics you can use to see if your video is connecting with your target audience. Check and record the statistics weekly at first, then monthly.

1. Insight for video, playlist, and channel
2. Time spent watching your video (duration is more important than the number of views)
3. Number of comments
4. Number of Likes
5. Number of Views (to compare between videos)

6. Number of shares and embeds
7. Number of new subscribers (YouTube friends usually ask to "friend" to sell you something)
8. Number of new and appropriate Facebook friends, Twitter followers, LinkedIn Connections

Create a spreadsheet and track the information. You will obtain a feel for how your style and message resonates with your following.

Promote Checklist

Let's see if you did everything you need to do to promote yourself and your video.

- ☑ Did you notify my following through all my social media outlets (email, Twitter, Facebook, YouTube, Blog, Squidoo)?
- ☑ Did you notify my not so socially connected outlets (post a notice on my bulletin board, window, cash register, voicemail)?
- ☑ Did you participate in conversations of other's blog posts?
- ☑ Did you Retweet and Follow Friday (#FF) my customers?
- ☑ Did you send a press release about a new playlist/series?
- ☑ Am you checking my statistics?

YOU DID IT! You finished the 7 P's <u>Viditude</u> Methodology. See how simple it is? Ready to do more?

Act 3: Final Thoughts for YOU

Every game has a post analysis of what worked and what didn't. It is a learning experience to help one improve for the next game. Your videos will be no different. This book is no different. Here are some final thoughts and resources to help you become the video star I know you will be.

Just Do It

This may seem overwhelming. Let me make it simple...JUST DO IT! Think about one video. Take each step in the 7 P process. Think ONLY about one process at a time. Spend 15 minutes a day concentrating on the video (I've written 9 books by <u>working on it at least 15 minutes a day</u>). Carry your camera and portable tripod with you at all times. Look at everything and think about how you could video the moment. After two weeks, you will be so much further along and the video-mountain won't seem so big. All it takes is believing you will increase your sales and knowing, with this book, YOU can do it! It's never been easier. The barrier to entry for you to tell and share your story has dropped with new products and the Internet. It's time for you to take advantage and ... JUST DO IT!

What's Next

Once you create and upload one video, you will realize how easy it is. It is time to think about what to do next.

Let's face it! The future of video is in the future of sharing information. More and more people will have access to the Internet (via PC/Mac, Tablet or Smartphone) to search and learn. This means you will see more and more video as a means of sharing information and creating an experience. The future of resource information is in video and multi-media presentations.

Think Style

Five different styles of videos were described. Try to create a video for each type. After creating a couple for each, you will uncover the video style you prefer. Then you can concentrate more on creating videos that fit that style and customer wants. Remember that a need does not necessitate a market.

Think about creating a few different testimonial videos and interchange them on your website and blog. Remember to remake testimonials. No testimonial should be more than 2 years old. Clothing, terms, and product changes need to be in sync with the video and the times.

Think Series

If your topic takes more than 5 minutes to explain, think about creating a series. If your product can be used in multiple ways, think about creating a series. Each series should have its own playlist. Customize your YouTube channel to show all your playlists. Remember to tag and describe each playlist. Let your audience know you will be uploading your videos, like a TV show, on a regular basis

(day of the week, month). Consistency builds trust. Develop a schedule you can live with and stick to it.

Think Product

Speakers know to record all their speeches. First, it provides great feedback to improve the speech and how it is delivered. More importantly, a video can be made into multiple products...which can be sold! You can create:

- ► an educational video series with a workbook
- ► a collection of related videos
- ► an audio version
- ► translated into a textbook (or a multi-media presentation, such as a <u>vook</u>)
- ► a webinar (or other multi-media educational format)
- ► live streaming of special events at your business

The above are just a few ideas to increase sales with material you have already created. Make sure, however, that you choose the full license for music and images which allows you to use them on items for sale!

Final to Do's:

1. Make sure you are on Facebook
    a. Have a personal page
    b. Create a business page off your personal page. Allow other employees to access and update the business page
    c. Create a page for every new book project or brand
2. Notify the search engines that you exist (including your website, blog, YouTube Channel, Facebook)
    a. Google: http://www.google.com/addurl/
    b. Yahoo: http://search.yahoo.com/info/submit.html
    c. Microsoft/Bing: http://www.bing.com/webmaster/submitsitepage.aspx
    d. An Independent Non-Profit: http://www.dmoz.org/help/submit.html

Call to Action

As with the closing of your video, we would like you to take action. We wholeheartedly encourage you to:

1. Write your core message...that **one** thing (remember Curly in City Slickers) or motive that drives **you** to do what you are doing.
2. Make a list of topics for videos.
3. Prioritize list.
4. Write the outline.
5. Write the closing.
6. Then, JUST DO IT!

Let us know how you are doing by <u>adding a comment about this book on our blog</u> and how it helped you or on our <u>Squidoo Viditude</u> lens.

Call to Action Video

(link address provided in Hyperlink Table at the end of the book)

Great Resources

This book doesn't contain everything. The video world is just changing too fast. My goal was to provide you enough information to help you get started. It was to provide you with basics which will remain important as the video world evolves.

Every day, videos are being watched. In fact, YouTube announced they average eight BILLION views a day. You can be a leader in your market, or you can let this train go without you. The choice is yours. You can be ahead of your competition or behind it. In fact, here's a great quote *from Project Change Management*, by Harrington, Conner, & Horney, McGraw-Hill, 2000: "You will be part of the parade. It's your choice whether you will be the bandleader, or come along after the parade has passed, sweeping up the horse droppings."

To continue building upon your knowledge and to get more ideas, I've provided a list of resources to continue growing your sales via video. This list changes and grows daily. Visit our <u>Viditude website</u> for the most current and up-to-date resources to help YOU demonstrate your value through video.

Websites to Remember

► Popular Video recorder's & lens:
- o http://www.store.Kodak.com
- o http://www.PhotoJojo.com/store/awesomeness/cell-phone-lenses/ (wide angle)
- o Camera Reviews: http://www.reviews.cnet.com/pocket-hd-camcorders/

► Popular Tripods:
- o http://www.joby.com/store (mini tripod & lighting)
- o http://www.dolica.com (tripods and camera bags)
- o Tripod Reviews:
  - ▪ http://www.intellireview.com
  - ▪ http://www.thedigitalcameraexperts.com/camera-tripod-reviews/

► Popular Audio Recorder and Microphones:
- o http://www.amazon.com/Sony-ICD-UX200RED-Digital-Recorder-Built/dp/B00387E5C6/ref=sr_1_2?ie=UTF8&s=electronics&qid=1290377826&sr=1-2
- o http://www.amazon.com/Olympus-Digital-Voice-Recorder-6200PC/dp/B002DSHMA8/ref=sr_1_3?s=electronics&ie=UTF8&qid=1290378040&sr=1-3
- o http://www.amazon.com/Zoom-Handy-Portable-Digital-Recorder/dp/B001QWBM62/ref=sr_1_1?s=electronics&ie=UTF8&qid=1303243088&sr=1-1

► Video Editing Software:
- o http://www.adobe.com/products/premiereel/
- o http://www.camtasia.com
- o http://www.campuppet.com
- o http://store.apple.com/us/product/MB642?afid=p2 19%7CMSUS&cid=OAS-US-KWM-AppleSoftware-US
- o *PC (highest rated):* Cyberlink http://www.cyberlink.com/products/powerdirector/overview_en_US.html
- o *PC (popular):* Vegas Movie Studio http://www.sonycreativesoftware.com/moviestudio hd/videoediting
- o *Mac:* ScreenFlow http://www.telestream.net/screen-flow/overview.htm
- o Editing Software Review: http://video-editing-software-review.toptenreviews.com/

► Audio Editing Software:
- o Audacity: http://www.Audacity.sourceforge.net
- o Levelator: http://www.conversationsnetwork.org/levelator

► Audio to Text Software (aka Speech Recognition):
- o Windows7 has software already included in the operating system
- o Dragon: http://www.nuance.com/talk/challenger.asp
- o Reviews: http://voice-recognition-software-review.toptenreviews.com/

► Royalty Free Music (<$30 each):
  o http://www.audiojungle.com
  o http://www.istockphoto.com
  o http://www.musicloops.com
  o http://www.productiontrax.com
  o http://www.shockwave-sound.com
  o http://www.sounddogs.com
  o http://www.stockmusic.net

► Royalty Free Photos:
  o http://www.123rf.com
  o http://www.istockphoto.com
  o http://www.photaki.com
  o http://www.shutterstock.com

► Backdrops (Muslin cotton fabric or digital to replace green screen or stand in front of while videoing):
  o Sample digital scenic backdrops (do a Google search) source: http://cart.owens-originals.com/category-s/117.htm
  o Sample hand painted backdrop (do a Google search) source: http://www.aurabackdrops.com/hand-painted-muslin-backdrops-c-2.html?page=1&sort=20a
  o Color Muslin fabric source (white provides a professional image): http://www.beaconfabric.com/vindex.html?cat242.htm
  o Natural and Bleached Muslin fabric source (you can dye your own or use it plain): http://www.dharmatrading.com/fabric/cotton/muslin.html

- o Inkjet transfers to iron your logo (choose by fabric):
  http://www.dharmatrading.com/html/eng/2935190
  -AA.shtml

► Miscellaneous Help:
  - o Get Published Information:
    http://www.squidoo.com/get-published
  - o Toastmasters: http://www.toastmasters.org
  - o Patricia Fripp: http://www.fripp.com
  - o Screenwriting Software: http://www.celtx.com
  - o Video Editing Help:
    - ▪ Pixability: http://www.pixability.com
    - ▪ Varvid: http://www.Varvid.com
    - ▪ Viditude: http://www.Viditude.com *(that's me)*

► **The Future of Video:**
  http://www.ted.com/talks/view/id/955

Books to Read

  ► *Beyond Viral* by Kevin Nalty
  ► *Get Seen* by Steve Garfield
  ► *Make a Good Script Great* by Linda Seger
  ► *Made To Stick* by Chip & Dan Heath
  ► *Presentation Zen* by Garr Reynolds
  ► *Purple Cow* by Seth Godin
  ► *Read This First* by Ron Ploff
  ► *Referral Engine* by John Jantsch
  ► *Start With Why* by Simon Sinek
  ► *Thank You Economy* by Gary Vaynerchuk
  ► *Yes!Attitude* by Jeffrey Gitomer

Websites To Grow Your Knowledge

▶ Video & Video Marketing Advice:
- o Maria A Andros: http://www.videomarketingqueen.com
- o Brendon Burchard: http://www.expertsacademy.com
- o Steve Garfield: http://stevegarfield.com/Site/Welcome.html
- o Jeff Martin: http://www.touchstorm.com
- o Pixability University: http://www.Pixability.com/university
- o Mark Robertson: http://www.reelseo.com/
- o Gideon Shalwick: http://www.gideonshalwick.com
- o Video Commerce Consortium: http://video-commerce.org/
- o Will Video For Food: http://www.willvideoforfood.com/

▶ General Business Advice:

- o Chris Keiff: http://www.1GoodReason.com
- o Patricia Fripp: http://www.Fripp.com
- o Jeffrey Gitomer: http://www.Gitomer.com
- o Media College: http://www.MediaCollege.com
- o Pat Ferdinandi: http://www.Viditude.com *(that's me)*
- o Seth Godin: http://www.SethGodin.com
- o Social Media Examiner: http://www.SocialMediaExaminer.com

o Toastmasters International: http://www.Toastmasters.org
o Alan Weiss: http://www.SummitConsulting.com

Hyperlink Reference Table

If you have purchased this book in a form without the ability to click on any of the hyperlinks, you will find the full URL in this hyperlink reference table. Only the hyperlinks not listed with the associated text are included.

Page	Reference	URL
	To Be Or Not To Be	http://www.youtube.com/watch?v=q3boJUTGJMI
	Viditude	http://www.viditude.com
vi	Patricia Fripp	http://www.fripp.com
vi	Steve Garfield	http://www.stevegarfield.com
vi	Jeffrey Gitomer	http://www.gitomer.com
vi	Seth Godin	http://www.sethgodin.com
vi	Kevin Naltz	http://www.willvideoforfood.com/
vi	Gideon Shalwick	http://www.gideonshadwick.com
vi	Alan Weiss	http://www.summitconsulting.com
1	Bird Lover's Only	http://www.birdloversonly.org
2	Back Street Boys	http://backstreetboys.com/
2	NY Times Flip Article	http://www.nytimes.com/2011/04/13/technology/13flip.html?_r=1&partner=rss&emc=rss
2	Snowball Video	http://www.youtube.com/watch?v=N7IZmRnAo6s
2	sulfur-crested cockatoo	http://www.youtube.com/watch?v=N7IZmRnAo6s
2	Snowball Video	http://www.youtube.com/watch?v=YIJf4ChKkQw

Page	Reference	URL
2	Snowball on CBS Sunday Morning	http://www.cbsnews.com/video/watch/?id=6554351n&tag=contentMain;contentBody
2	Snowball in Scientific Research Papers	http://www.birdloversonly.org/blscience.shtml
2	Snowball in Taco Bell Commercial	http://www.youtube.com/watch?v=5pCoSwbcBNU
2	Snowball T-Shirts	http://www.birdloversonly.org/blshirt.shtml
2	Bird Lover's Only Charity	http://www.birdloversonly.org
3	Facebook	http://www.facebook.com
3	Twitter	http://www.Twitter.com
3	Squidoo	http://www.Squidoo.com
3	LinkedIn	http://www.LinkedIn.com
3	FourSquare	http://www.FourSqure.com
3	SlideShare	http://www.SlideShare.com
3	Flickr	http://www.Flickr.com
3	YouTube	http://www.YouTube.com
5	53 times	http://www.businessweek.com/technology/content/feb2009/tc20090212_136831.htm – article
5	Click-through rate	http://www.eweek.com/c/a/Midmarket/Video-Emails-Increase-Clickthrough-Rates-Study-Shows-816653/
5	YouTube search engine	http://www.tgdaily.com/trendwatch-features/39777-youtube-surpasses-yahoo-as-world%E2%80%99s-2-search-engine
5	Chitika study	http://insights.chitika.com/2010/the-value-of-google-result-positioning/
5	Chitika	http://chitika.com/com/
5	Social Media Week 2011	http://socialmediaweek.org/newyork/

Page	Reference	URL
5	MeFeedia	http://www.mefeedia.com/
5	Viditude	http://www.viditude.com
5	Viditude 7 P's	http://viditude.com/how-we-help-you/
8	Write a book playlist	http://www.youtube.com/view_play_list?p=6F929F151400D17B
9	Amazon	http://www.amazon.com
10	Email Viditude	mailto:TalkToUs@Viditude.com
14	Simon Sinek	http://www.simonsinek.com/
14	Order Start With Why	http://www.amazon.com/exec/obidos/ASIN/1591842808/stratebusinedeci/
14	Simon Sinek Start With Why video	http://www.youtube.com/watch?v=qp0HIF3SfI4&feature=player_embedded
15	City Slickers	http://www.imdb.com/title/tt0101587/
19	AARP	http://www.aarp.org/
21	Early adopters	http://en.wikipedia.org/wiki/Diffusion_of_innovations
22	Squeeze Page	http://en.wikipedia.org/wiki/Squeeze_page
22	Orabreath Video	http://www.youtube.com/user/curebadbreath
22	Pest Plus Testimonial Video	http://www.youtube.com/watch?v=yVxu3QS0RX8
22	Pest Plus	http://www.PestPlus.net
23	Self-Improvement Mentor	http://www.self-improvement-mentor.com/list-of-human-emotions.html
24	Patricia Fripp	http://www.Fripp.com
24	Patricia Fripp	http://www.Fripp.com
25	One Sentence Video	http://www.youtube.com/watch?v=sBWlfYDTiR0
25	Daniel Pink	http://www.danielpink.com

Page	Reference	URL
28	Jeffrey Gitomer Powerful Questions Video	http://www.youtube.com/watch ?v=uxEZqQBVAXA
28	Gitomer	http://www.gitomer.com/
28	TED	http://www.ted.com/
28	Hans Rosling TED Presentation	http://www.ted.com/talks/hans _rosling_asia_s_rise_how_and_ when.html
29	Hans Rosling	http://www.ted.com/speakers/h ans_rosling.html
29	Garr Reynolds Presentation Zen	http://www.presentiationzen.co m/
29	Presentation Zen Book	http://www.amazon.com/exec/o bidos/ASIN/0321525655/strateb usinedeci/
29	Jeffrey Gitomer	http://www.gitomer.com
35	Amazon	http://www.Amazon.com
42	Bird Lover's Only Charity	http://www.birdloversonly.org
42	Snowball Video	http://www.youtube.com/watch ?v=YIJf4ChKkQw
43	Linda Seger	http://www.lindaseger.com/inde x.html
52	Patricia Fripp	http://www.fripp.com
52	Garr Reynolds	http://www.presentationzen.co m
52	Toastmasters	http://www.toastmasters.org
52	Jeffrey Gitomer	http://www.gitomer.com
52	Seth Godin	http://www.sethgodin.com
52	Les Brown	http://www.lesbrown.com
55	Billy Mays	http://en.wikipedia.org/wiki/Bill y_mays
56	FedEx Commercial	http://www.youtube.com/watch ?v=NeK5ZjtpO-M
58	Toyota Swagger Video	http://www.youtube.com/result s?search_query=toyota+swagg er+wagon+commercial&aq=1

Page	Reference	URL
61	Steve Garfield	http://www.stevegarfield.com
61	Get Seen	http://www.amazon.com/exec/obidos/ASIN/0470525460/stratebusinedeci/
62	Google	http://www.google.com
62	WebEx	http://www.webex.com
62	Go To Meeting	http://www.gotomeeting.com/fec/
62	Skype	http://www.skype.com/intl/en-us/home
63	Finding 15 Minutes Spoof	http://www.youtube.com/watch?v=6GRihq1t_MU
67	Steve Garfield	http://www.stevegarfield.com
68	Enterprise Architecture Video	http://www.youtube.com/watch?v=W-IHxUUH8I8
74	Get Published Episode 1	http://www.youtube.com/watch?v=i8RUSUVjgy4
75	Awakenings	http://www.imdb.com/title/tt0099077/
75	Toastmasters	http://www.toastmasters.org
72	Happy Feet	http://www.imdb.com/title/tt0366548/
77	Jeffrey Gitomer	http://www.gitomer.com
77	Jodi Kaplan	http://www.kaplancopy.com/
78	How To Get Published Interview with Jodi Kaplan	http://www.youtube.com/watch?v=yXxPDj-uKlg
79	Campuppet	http://www.campuppet.com/
82	Le Sportsac	http://www.lesportsac.com/store/7627_5205.html
82	Jeffrey Gitomer	http://www.gitomer.com
83	Billy Mays	http://en.wikipedia.org/wiki/Billy_mays
84	Mrs. Doubtfire	http://www.imdb.com/title/tt0107614/
85	180 degree rule	http://en.wikipedia.org/wiki/180_degree_rule

Page	Reference	URL
89	Gitomer YouTube	http://www.youtube.com/buygitomer
89	Alan Weiss	http://www.summitconsulting.com
89	Writing On The Wall	http://summitconsulting.com/video/writing-on-the-wall-episode-53.php
90	Patricia Fripp	http://www.fripp.com
91	Scarlet's Feathers	http://www.scarletsfeathers.com
91	Library of Congress	http://www.loc.gov/index.html
91	Typewriter Eraser Sculpture	http://www.nga.gov/feature/sculpturegarden/sculpture/index.shtm
91	Get Published Information Page	http://www.squidoo.com/get-published
94	Get Published Episode 21	http://www.youtube.com/watch?v=cIrbFFcEHDA
94	Get Published Playlist	http://www.youtube.com/view_play_list?p=6F929F151400D17B
94	Viditude	http://www.Viditude.com
95	Get Published Episode 26	http://www.youtube.com/watch?v=xhkrTEwWZKo
96	Creative Commons Description	http://en.wikipedia.org/wiki/Creative_Commons
96	Audio Jungle License Explanation	http://audiojungle.net/wiki/support/legal-terms/licensing-terms/
101	YouTube	http://www.youtube.com
101	Tubler	http://www.tubler.com
101	TubeMogul	http://www.TubeMogul
101	Blip.tv	http://www.blip.tv.com
101	Vimeo	http://www.vimeo.com
101	Viddler	http://www.viddler.com

Page	Reference	URL
101	Order Get Seen by Steve Garfield	http://www.amazon.com/exec/obidos/ASIN/0470525460/stratebusinedeci/
101	Amazon S3	http://aws.amazon.com/s3/
106	Get Published Playlist	http://www.youtube.com/view_play_list?p=6F929F151400D17B
106	Strategic Business Decisions YouTube Channel	http://www.YouTube.com/SBDiPat
106	Viditude YouTube Channel	http://www.YouTube.com/Viditude
108	YouTube How To Add Annotations Tutorial	http://www.youtube.com/watch?v=XXtwUrKwK3g&feature=fvw
108	YouTube How To Use Insight Tutorial	http://www.youtube.com/watch?v=Xo6HBKTyIzQ
110	Facebook	http://www.facebook.com
110	LinkedIn	http://www.LinkedIn.com
110	Mari Smith	https://www.facebook.com/marismith
111	Viditude YouTube Channel	http://www.YouTube.com/Viditude
112	Ant's Eye View	http://www.antseyeview.com/
112	Ant's Eye View Social Media Engagement Evaluation	http://www.antseyeview.com/wp-content/uploads/2011/01/AEV-Social-Engagement-Journey-Assessment.pdf
113	RSS Description	http://en.wikipedia.org/wiki/Web_feed
113	How To Create a YouTube RSS Feed/API	http://youtu.be/l7xcMhpgBic
114	1 Good Reason	http://www.1goodreason.com/

Page	Reference	URL
114	1 Good Reason "Like" explanation	http://www.1goodreason.com/blog/blog/2010/12/10/two-stupid-facebook-like-buttons/#more-1342
116	Snowball Material	http://www.birdloversonly.org/blbuy.shtml
116	Bird Lover's Only Charity	http://www.birdloversonly.org/
116	Bird Talk Magazine	http://www.birdchannel.com/bird-magazines/bird-talk/default.aspx
116	Get Published Video Series	http://www.youtube.com/sbdipat#g/c/6F929F151400D17B
117	Field Of Dreams	http://www.imdb.com/title/tt0097351/
118	Don Snyder The Idea Guy	http://dontheideaguy.com/archives/1329
118	Gary Vaynerchuk	http://garyvaynerchuk.com/
118	Order Crush It	http://www.amazon.com/exec/obidos/ASIN/0061914177/stratebusinedeci/
118	Order The Thank You Economy	http://www.amazon.com/exec/obidos/ASIN/0061914185/stratebusinedeci/
118	GaryVee Twitter	http://www.twitter.com/garyvee
118	Watch Gary V Book Signing Talk	http://www.youtube.com/view_play_list?p=ECB7BDCA57E5F280
119	Marketing Curve	http://en.wikipedia.org/wiki/Diffusion_of_innovations
119	Ron Ploff	http://ronamok.com/
121	Constant Contact	http://www.constantcontact.com
121	Ace of Sales	http://www.aceofsales.com
121	Jeffrey Gitomer Sales Caffeine Registration	http://www.gitomer.com/sales-magazine/Sales-Caffeine.html

Page	Reference	URL
121	Real SEO	http://www.reelseo.com/facebook-video-marketing/
123	How To Create a Facebook Landing Page	http://www.youtube.com/watch?annotation_id=annotation_787677&feature=iv&v=rr_brmunCJc
124	Squidoo	http://www.squidoo.com
124	Get Published Squidoo Landing Page	http://www.squidoo.com/get-published
124	Social Oomph	http://www.socialoomph.com/
124	Hoot Suite	http://www.hootsuite.com/
125	Jeffrey Gitomer Sales Caffeine Registration	http://www.gitomer.com/sales-magazine/Sales-Caffeine.html
125	mRSS	http://en.wikipedia.org/wiki/MRSS
125	Video Sitemap	http://www.google.com/support/webmasters/bin/topic.py?topic=10079
125	Video Sitemap	http://www.google.com/webmasters/videositemaps/
125	Format Description	https://www.google.com/support/webmasters/bin/answer.py?hl=en&answer=80472#4
126	Google Video Sitemap Wordpress Plugin	http://wordpress.org/extend/plugins/xml-sitemaps-for-videos/
128	United Breaks Guitars Video	http://youtu.be/5YGc4zOqozo
128	Dave Carroll	http://www.davecarrollmusic.com/
128	Taylor Guitars Response Video	http://youtu.be/n12WFZq2__0
130	Help A Reporter Sign Up	http://helpareporter.com/
130	Google Adwords	http://www.google.com/intl/en/ads/

Page	Reference	URL
130	Facebook Ads	http://www.facebook.com/advertising/?campaign_id=194417723019&placement=exact&creative=5811896912&keyword=facebook+ads&extra_1=0a4e55c3-74d0-f389-1a5c-0000340d3bf1
131	Social Oomph	http://www.socialoomph.com/
131	Hoot Suite	http://www.hootsuite.com/
132	Viditude	http://www.viditude.com
132	1 Good Reason	http://www.1goodreason.com
132	Becky Blanton	http://www.beckyblanton.com/
132	Jodi Kaplan	http://www.kaplancopy.com
132	Pixability	http://www.pixability.com
132	Viditude	http://www.viditude.com
134	Jeffrey Gitomer	http://www.gitomer.com
135	Viditude	http://www.viditude.com
136	Finding 15 mins	http://www.youtube.com/watch?v=i8RUSUVjgy4
140	Vook	http://www.vook.com
140	Viditude Blog	http://www.viditude.com
140	Viditude Squidoo Lens	http://www.squidoo.com/viditude
140	Call To Action Video	http://www.youtube.com/watch?v=pYqC1QXOH2I
141	Viditude	http://www.viditude.com
145	Beyond Viral	http://www.amazon.com/exec/obidos/ASIN/0470598883/stratebusinedeci/
145	Get Seen	http://www.amazon.com/exec/obidos/ASIN/0470525460/stratebusinedeci/
145	Make A Good Script Great	http://www.amazon.com/exec/obidos/ASIN/0573699216/stratebusinedeci/
145	Made to Stick	http://www.amazon.com/exec/obidos/ASIN/1400064287/stratebusinedeci/

Page	Reference	URL
145	Presentation Zen	http://www.amazon.com/exec/obidos/ASIN/0321525655/stratebusinedeci/
145	Purple Cow	http://www.amazon.com/exec/obidos/ASIN/1591843170/stratebusinedeci/
145	Read This First	http://www.amazon.com/exec/obidos/ASIN/1440166854/stratebusinedeci/
145	Referral Engine	http://www.amazon.com/exec/obidos/ASIN/1591843111/stratebusinedeci/
145	Start with Why	http://www.amazon.com/exec/obidos/ASIN/1591842808/stratebusinedeci/
145	Thank You Economy	http://www.amazon.com/exec/obidos/ASIN/0061914185/stratebusinedeci/
145	Yes Attitude	http://www.amazon.com/exec/obidos/ASIN/0131986473/stratebusinedeci/
162	Graditude Video	http://www.youtube.com/watch?v=9HcSxKBggpE
163	The Oasis Bird Sanctuary	http://the-oasis.org/donatenow.php
163	World Parrot Trust	http://www.parrots.org/donate
163	The Alex Foundation	http://alexfoundation.org/donate.html
163	Birds Lovers Only	http://www.birdloversonly.org/
165	Vook	http://www.vook.com
166	Viditude Testimonials	http://www.youtube.com/watch?v=6Md3qm44cu0
168	Inspirational Closing	http://youtu.be/JuuCU0DuFAs

Testimonial Release Form

Here is an example of a testimonial release form. You will need a separate one for each testimonial. You will also need one for any interviewee. If you are a B2B type company and are interviewing their customers but may wish to use the video, you will need another release form from the company as well as his or her customers.

The undersigned ("Testimonial Provider") enters into this Agreement with _____ and _____ ("Producer"). I have been informed and understand that the Producer is producing a videotape program and that my name, likeness, image, voice, appearance and/or performance are being recorded and made a part of that production.

1. I, the Testimonial Provider, grant the Producer and its designees the right to use my name, likeness, image voice, appearance, and performance as embodied in the Product whether recorded on or transferred to videotape, film, slides, photographs, audio tapes, or other media, now known or later developed. This grant includes without limitation the right to edit, mix or duplicate and to use or re-use the Product in whole or part as the Producer may elect. The Producer or its designee shall have complete ownership of the Product in which I appear, including copyright interests, and I acknowledge

that I have no interest or ownership in the Product or its copyright.

2. I also grant the Producer and its designees the right to broadcast, exhibit, market, sell and otherwise distribute the Product, either in whole or in part, and either alone or with other Products, for internal use, closed-circuit exhibition, home video distribution or any other purpose that the Producer or its designees in their sole discretion may determine. This grant includes the right to use the Product for promoting or publicizing any of the uses.

3. I confirm that I have the right to enter into this Agreement, that I am not restricted by any commitments to their parties, and that the Producer has no financial commitment or obligations to me as a result of this Agreement. I hereby give all clearances, copyright and otherwise, for use of my name likeness, image voice, appearance, and performance embodied in the Product. I expressly release and indemnify the Producer and its officers, employees, agents and designees from any and all claims known and unknown arising out of or in any way connected with the above granted uses and representations. The rights granted the Producer herein are perpetual and worldwide.

4. In consideration of all the above, I hereby acknowledge receipt of reasonable and fair consideration from the Producer.

I have read the foregoing and understand its terms and stipulations and agree to all of them:

Testimonial Provider's Name (Please Print):
_____

Signature:
_____

Date: _____

(If the person signing is under age 18, a parent or legal guardian must sign below.)
I hereby certify that I am the parent or legal guardian of the Testimonial Provider named above and I give my consent without reservation to the foregoing on behalf of him or her.
Signature of Parent or Guardian:
_____

Date: _____

When You Need Help

Hey, Viditude love to learn about different businesses and want to help you to succeed! We are here to help you. Here are different ways to get in touch with us:

- ▶ Direct:
  - o Call me at 973-509-9427
  - o Email me either at:
    - ▪ TalkToUs@Viditude.com
    - ▪ PatF@Viditude.com
  - o Physical Mailing Address:
    - ▪ PO Box 638 Montclair NJ 07042

- ▶ Join the Viditude community:
  - o Viditude.com
  - o Facebook.com/Viditude
  - o Squidoo.com/Viditude
  - o YouTube.com/user/Viditude
  - o LinkedIn.com/in/PatFerdinandi
  - o Twitter.com/Viditude   (or my personal Twitter account: @ThoughtTrans)

Gratitude

Thank you for reading, listening, and watching this book. May the information you learned bring you lots of new opportunities to connect with your community.

I   **Play the Graditude Video**

(link address provided in Hyperlink Table at the end of the book)

▶ Did you learn something to save you time?

▶ Did you learn something to help your business?

▶ Did you learn something to help you communicate more effectively with your community?

▶ Did you learn how to demonstrate your value through video?

If you answered yes to any of these questions, please consider helping a charity of your choice. If you do not have a specific charity in mind, thank a parrot by donating a little to help them thrive. Click on the logo for the parrot organization of your choice to make your donation. Tell them Scarlet sent you.

The Oasis Sanctuary	World Parrot Trust	The Alex Foundation	Bird Lovers Only

About Viditude

making sure your videos are creating a lot of talk.

You have specialists in marketing, videoing, and social media. What's missing for most is a strategist. A strategist is a key person who brings it all together in a strategy to combine video and social media.

With the ability to take your own videos, how do you use this wonderful opportunity to demonstrate your best? How do you make sure you come across well and connect on video? It can be confusing and intimidating if you do not know how to talk to the camera, how to set a stage, how to recognize and edit rambling dialog into concise words and still be entertaining enough to have your customers watch you from beginning to end.

Viditude has the skills to help you prepare, produce, and promote *you*. With video, our goals are:

▶ To find ways to connect to your potential customers; converting them to real customers.
▶ To help you increase revenue and market share.
▶ To demonstrating your value through video.

About The Author

I call myself a *Chief Thought Translator* because I help convert **YOUR** ideas into something to help **YOU** make more revenue. My enthusiasm and creative mind add a touch of levity to make every interaction a friendly and productive one. The ideas and suggestions I share are always focused on helping **YOU** to succeed. After all, it's not a transaction but a relationship! Allow me the opportunity to help **YOU** by being your video strategist.

My unique combinations of skills are available to help you succeed. I draw on my experience as a public speaker, trainer, screenwriter, published author, and business management consultant to address your need. Areas I can help you include engaging through video with people not like you, expanding your market, and becoming flexible for change. As an entrepreneur, I have successfully built both service and product-based small companies (with the assistance of Scarlet) involving photography, graphic design and video skills.

Do I know about social media? Well, I've authored multiple blogs, articles, chapters, books and have written in the new book style that will hopefully culminate in a Vook (video book). I've been published by McGraw-Hill,

American Management Association and Addison-Wesley. I continually self-publish and use digital media (blogs, Facebook, LinkedIn, Twitter, eZines, and videos) to share my knowledge with individuals and businesses just like yours.

How can this help **YOU**? I mentor and inspire others with my story-telling speeches and insights into today's digital world. With my combination of social media knowledge, business sense, strategy, and planning; I can help your business:

- ► come up with ideas that help you succeed,
- ► provide a customized plan to help them reach your goals,
- ► hold your hand through mentoring, and/or
- ► help you produce what you need.

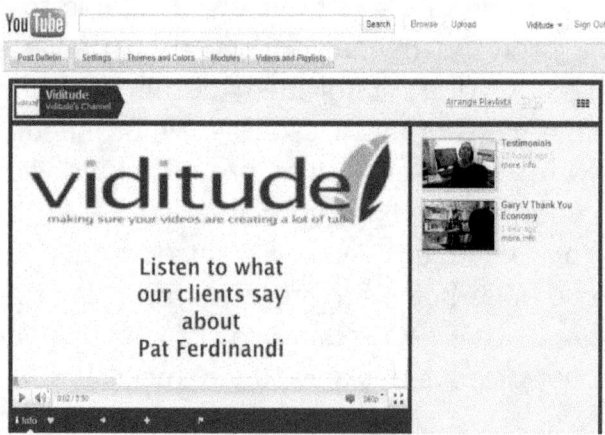

Viditude Testimonials
Watch Pat Ferdinandi's video testimonial.
(link address provided in Hyperlink Table at the end of the book)

So, who is Pat Ferdinandi? Well, Mark Twain squawked it best:

> She was not quite what you would call refined.
> She was not quite what you would call unrefined.
> She was the kind of person that keeps a parrot.
> *~ Following the Equator;*
> *Pudd'nhead Wilson's New Calendar*

I'm different. I'm engaging. I know what I'm talking about and am willing to share it with **YOU**. Don't believe me? Watch what others are squawkin' about my abilities.

If you hear a squawk in the background, you are hearing Scarlet, a Solomon Island Eclectus Parrot. You will see and hear her in many of my videos.

Final Checklist

- ☑ JUST DO IT
- ☑ DO IT AGAIN
- ☑ Email <u>PatF@Viditude.com</u> or call 973-509-9427 for help
- ☑ Keep this book for ideas, references, and to remind yourself to

JUST   DO   IT!

Your Video Playbook Inspirational Closing

(link address provided in Hyperlink Table at the end of the book)

Paraphrased from Hamlet by William Shakespeare:

Neither a straggler nor fearful be;

For thou be successful only by doing,

And cowardliness dulls the edge of presence

This above all: to thine ownself be true,

And it must follow, as the night the day,

Thou can be successful by producing video

Thank you for reading, watching, and listening!

www.ingramcontent.com/pod-product-compliance
Lightning Source LLC
Chambersburg PA
CBHW051517170526
45165CB00002B/506